RICCARDO MUTI
Twenty Years in Philadelphia

RICCARDO MUTI

Twenty Years in Philadelphia

RICCARDO MUTI: TWENTY YEARS IN PHILADELPHIA

Copyright © 1992 by The Philadelphia Orchestra Association
1420 Locust Street
Philadelphia, PA 19102
Joseph Neubauer, Chairman
Joseph H. Kluger, President
Judith Frankfurt, General Manager
Diana Burgwyn, Director of Public Relations

Editor: Judith Karp Kurnick
Associate Editor: Leah Krauss
Production Manager: Jean E. Brubaker

Design and Typography: Russell Hassell NYC
Printed by: Indian Valley Printing Limited, Souderton, PA

ACKNOWLEDGEMENTS

Discography research courtesy of *Musica* magazine, Milan

For photographic research: Anne Sears, Westminster Choir College; Ann Diebold, The Curtis Institute of Music; EMI Classics, London
For editorial support: Cathy Barbash, JoAnne Barry, Suzanna Bernd, Mary Lou Falcone, David Glassman, Bernard Jacobson, Nica Lewis, Cristina Muti, Mimi O'Malley, Paul Orlando, Gianne Conard Sell, Richard Wernick, Vera Wilson
For use of Shapey Symphonie concertante: Theodore A. Presser, Inc.

PHOTOGRAPHY

Bob Adler 47; Laird Bindrim 1, 25, 54, 55 (top and middle), 71, 76 (bottom), 77; Jean E. Brubaker 4, 19, 26, 31, 32, 34 (bottom), 35, 37 (top), 39, 41, 43, 45 (bottom), 46, 48, 49, 55 (middle), 56, 61, 64 (top), 70, 72 (top and bottom), 73, 74 (top), 94 (bottom), 95 (top), 96 (top and bottom), 97, 99, 100; Diana Burgwyn 65 (top), 95 (bottom), 102; Larry French 40; Friedrich 59; Judy Geist 55 (bottom), 87, 89, 93 (top); Spud Grammar 42 (bottom); Matthew Griendling 36; Louis Hood 10, 57 (bottom) 86 (bottom), 88, 92 (top), 101; Judith Karp Kurnick 65 (bottom), 66, 68, 69, 92 (bottom); Amy Layman 42 (top), 78 (bottom); Lelli & Masotti 15, 20, 82; Meyer 67; Steven Mullen 80; Pfaff 52; Jules Schick 75; Steve J. Sherman 13, 17, 34 (top), 45 (top), 50, 61 (top); Adrian Siegel 14, 37 (bottom); Terry's Photography 64 (bottom); Don Tracy 81 (top); Robert Walker 74 (bottom); Ed Wheeler 84, 91; Gerald Williams (*The Philadelphia Inquirer*) 16; Reg Wilson (EMI Classics) 34 (middle); Sharon Wohlmuth (*The Philadelphia Inquirer*) 76 (top); Liz Wuillermin 94 (top).

OPENING LETTERS

RICCARDO MUTI WITH PHILADELPHIA ORCHESTRA
ASSOCIATION CHAIRMAN AND CEO JOSEPH NEUBAUER
(R.) AND PRESIDENT AND COO JOSEPH KLUGER (L.).

The
Philadelphia
Orchestra

RICCARDO MUTI,
MUSIC DIRECTOR

When an orchestra and a conductor have been together for two decades, as has been the case with Riccardo Muti and The Philadelphia Orchestra, it is easy to take for granted the high level of artistry that they have achieved. We began this book as a way of reflecting on their accomplishments together and of showing our esteem and affection for Maestro Muti. Such a volume, we felt, would concretely document his time with the Orchestra under his leadership as guest conductor, Principal Guest Conductor, and, since 1980, as Music Director.

But the book has ended as something more: a vivid collection of shared memories and a source of renewed pride about the international artistic stature of The Philadelphia Orchestra. What follows is a portrait of a Riccardo Muti of many facets and talents. Many of you may know about the serious leader of musicians, with a clear artistic vision and uncompromising standards. But what has also emerged is a picture of the man, whose conducting philosophy is to make music <u>with</u> musicians; the nurturer of young talent; the confidant and counselor to many; the impeccable judge of character; and the private man, with a warm sense of humor shared with those fortunate enough to have worked with him.

We invite you to share in the celebration of these twenty glorious years and hope you enjoy the memories captured in this book. On behalf of the Board, musicians, staff, and Volunteer Committees of The Philadelphia Orchestra Association, we extend heartfelt gratitude to Maestro Muti for sharing these years with us. As he ends his tenure as Music Director, it is deeply satisfying to know that our relationship with him will continue as he assumes the role of Laureate Conductor.

Joseph Neubauer
Chairman and Chief Executive Officer

Joseph H. Kluger
President and Chief Operating Officer

1420 Locust Street
Philadelphia, PA 19102
(215) 893-1900

Cable: PHILAORCH
TWX: PHILAORCH PHA 7106701048
FAX: (215) 893-1948

Commonwealth of Pennsylvania

Governor's Office

TO: MAESTRO RICCARDO MUTI

It is with a mixture of sadness and gratitude that I bid farewell to you as musical director of the Philadelphia Orchestra. During your tenure in Philadelphia, you have brought great honor and esteem to our Commonwealth. Your musical genius has elevated an already great orchestra to a new level of artistic excellence that is recognized worldwide, and you have set new standards for players, composers and audiences alike.

I am especially pleased that I was able to recognize your contribution to the cultural life of Pennsylvania through the 1989 Governor's Award for Excellence in the Arts. Your statement that artists have historically been among the most influential and deeply involved members of society has stayed with me since that time.

On behalf of all Pennsylvanians, I thank you for your inspiring presence in our Commonwealth and your brilliant leadership of the Philadelphia Orchestra.

Best wishes for your continuing success.

Robert P. Casey
Governor

17th December, 1991

My Dear Maestro,

Today we pay tribute to your association, stretching over two decades, with the glorious Philadelphia Orchestra.

I am particularly glad to convey to you, on this memorable occasion, the greetings of the Italian Government and my most heartfelt personal ones. These feelings of gratitude are shared by all our countrymen, by the millions of Americans of Italian heritage, and by the multitude of music lovers throughout the world.

Your passionate energy and your immense natural talent are matched by rigorous professionalism and a rare gift for research and study. What you have done and still do to bring back to life forgotten scores of great beauty is no less important than your extraordinary achievements in the art of musical conducting.

Our deep regret is that at the end of this season you will be leaving your position of Music Director of the Philadelphia Orchestra. But the links with the Orchestra will remain since you have been appointed Laureate Conductor; and we are sure that you will frequently return to this city which has such an outstanding musical tradition and has been enriched, thanks to you, by the presence of one of the greatest conductors ever.

Yours

United States Senate
WASHINGTON, DC 20510-3802

April 22, 1992

Riccardo Muti
Maestro
The Philadelphia Orchestra
Philadelphia, Pennsylvania

Dear Maestro:

With your legion of fans and admirers, I congratulate you on your 20 years with The Philadelphia Orchestra. And while I lament the fact that you will be stepping down as Music Director at the conclusion of the 1991-1992 season, I find consolation in that you will remain with the Orchestra as Laureate Conductor and will return frequently in that capacity.

The Philadelphia Orchestra was widely regarded as the finest in the music world when you became its Music Director. I believe it continues to be the best, and you are responsible for maintaining this preeminence.

As a Philadelphian, I am immensely proud of The Philadelphia Orchestra and its well-deserved international reputation. You have been a part of that for the past two decades and we are all in your debt.

Yours has been a brilliant career. I know it will continue to be one. I wish you the very best in all future endeavors. But please remember Philadelphia and come back as often as you can.

Sincerely,

Arlen Specter

HARRIS WOFFORD
PENNSYLVANIA

ENVIRONMENT AND PUBLIC WORKS
FOREIGN RELATIONS
SMALL BUSINESS

United States Senate

WASHINGTON, DC 20510-3803

December 12, 1991

Maestro Riccardo Muti
Music Director
The Philadelphia Orchestra
1420 Locust Street
Philadelphia, Pennsylvania 19102

Dear Maestro Muti:

As you mark your twentieth year with The Philadelphia Orchestra, first as Guest Conductor, then as Principal Guest Conductor, and finally as Music Director, it is with regret that we will see your tenure as Music Director come to an end at the conclusion of the 1991-1992 season.

Millions throughout the Delaware Valley, our Commonwealth, our country and the world have been fortunate through the years to enjoy one of the world's finest orchestras under your baton. While one phase of your association with The Philadelphia Orchestra draws to a close, music lovers everywhere look forward to your future role as Laureate Conductor.

It is fitting that we celebrate both the past two decades of your leadership of The Philadelphia Orchestra and the years ahead in which we look forward to your continued association and contributions that bring pride to the city of Philadelphia and our Commonwealth.

Bravo!

Sincerely,

Harris Wofford

Harris Wofford

1980: PHILADELPHIA'S CITY HALL
DISPLAYS A WELCOME BANNER.

WELCOME
RICCARDO MUTI
MUSIC DIRECTOR
THE PHILADELPHIA ORCHESTRA

CITY OF PHILADELPHIA

EDWARD G. RENDELL
MAYOR

February 5, 1992

Maestro Riccardo Muti
The Philadelphia Orchestra
1420 Locust Street
Philadelphia, PA 19102

Dear Maestro Muti:

As Mayor of the City of Philadelphia, I have distinctly mixed feelings about marking your 20th anniversary with The Philadelphia Orchestra.

Of course, I am delighted to pay tribute to your two decades with our world-class orchestra, the last 12 of which were spent as Music Director. But I am equally saddened by your departure.

It is my hope that you will again grace our fair city with your presence and your magnificent talent.

Sincerely,

Edward G. Rendell

A PROFILE

When Riccardo Muti came to Philadelphia at age thirty-one, he had already been Music Director of Florence's Maggio Musicale for three years, and soon after his first guest appearances here in 1972, he was appointed Principal Conductor of the Philharmonia Orchestra in London. He had already conducted the Berlin Philharmonic and at the Salzburg Festival. But Philadelphia was the site of his North American debut, and we like to think we somehow "discovered" this prodigious young talent.

Each of Muti's earliest responsibilities proved to be a cornerstone on which was built a major aspect of his international career. As William Weaver describes in his essay, Muti's thirteen years at the Maggio Musicale gave him a reputation in Italy for outstanding work in opera, which eventually led to his 1986 appointment as Music Director of La Scala, Milan. From the earliest successes in Salzburg with the Vienna Philharmonic and in Berlin, there has been a strong bond with these institutions in both vocal and symphonic repertoire, a bond that Derek Weber of the *Salzburger Nachtrichten* discusses here in greater detail.

What is easy for Americans to miss, however, is the sheer profile of this artist abroad. In Italy, the opening of La Scala every December 7 is a national event, something on the order of our Super Bowl. It is a political event as well, and Muti has created controversy with new productions of works not often heard there. Each time they succeed, he becomes more of a national hero.

In Salzburg he is one of many international artists who take part in the rarefied musical and social atmosphere of the festival. Yet he is the one the Vienna Philharmonic chose to conduct its recordings of the complete Mozart symphonies.

In Japan, where Muti has appeared often with Philadelphia, La Scala, and other orchestras, a group of loyal admirers began a Muti fan club some years back, developing their own newsletter and a regular following across the country.

Let us remember that an artist is the sum of all of his activities, and begin to understand more about him as we look at some of those outside Philadelphia.

Riccardo Muti: A Biography

by Bernard Jacobson

Riccardo Muti conducted The Philadelphia Orchestra for the first time on October 27, 1972, at the invitation of Eugene Ormandy, who had heard him in rehearsal during an Orchestra visit to Florence. Muti's impact on Philadelphia was such that in 1977 he was appointed Principal Guest Conductor, and in 1980 he succeeded Ormandy as Music Director. His twelve-year term has constituted a virtuoso partnership acclaimed around the world. Attendance at the Orchestra's subscription series in Philadelphia and New York has reached new highs, and several critics in the United States and abroad have judged The Philadelphia Orchestra under Muti to be America's premier orchestra. Muti and the Orchestra have toured extensively together in the United States, Asia, Europe, and South America.

During his term as Music Director, Maestro Muti has reactivated The Philadelphia Orchestra's tradition of versatility by introducing new music from all periods to its audiences, and has captured the imagination of young people by opening dress rehearsals to high-school students. He appointed Richard Wernick consultant for contemporary music, and to succeed Mr. Wernick he appointed another Pulitzer Prize-winning American composer, Bernard Rands, composer in residence with the sponsorship of the Meet the Composer Orchestra Residencies Program. Muti's and the Orchestra's leading role in championing new American music earned ASCAP awards in 1987 and again in 1991.

Maestro Muti's 1983 revival of the Orchestra's operatic tradition was greeted by critics internationally as an important and exciting development. Their concert performances of operas by Gluck, Wagner, Verdi, and Puccini have taken their place among the seasons' most memorable events, and continued with the recent presentation of Leoncavallo's *Pagliacci,* featuring Luciano Pavarotti. Many of the Orchestra's recordings with Muti for Angel/EMI have won international awards. They include the first Beethoven symphony cycle by an American orchestra to be recorded for compact disc. Recent seasons have also seen the initiation of a relationship with Philips Classics, beginning with a Brahms cycle, and the recording of 20th-century American music for New World Records.

Born in Naples in 1941, Riccardo Muti was Music Director of the Maggio Musicale in Florence from 1969 to 1982. In 1972 he appeared in London with the Philharmonia Orchestra, making so favorable an impression that he was appointed to succeed Otto Klemperer as Principal Conductor. In 1979 the post of Music Director (at that time a rarity in London musical life) was created for him. On relinquishing it in 1982, he was honored by the players

During a 1989 tour of the Soviet Union with La Scala, Riccardo and Cristina Muti are greeted by Soviet President Mikhail Gorbachev and his wife Raisa.

with the title Conductor Laureate. He became Music Director of La Scala, Milan, in 1986 while continuing his Philadelphia post. With La Scala he has toured Japan and performed Verdi's Requiem at Notre Dame in Paris before a vast audience both inside and (through closed-circuit television) outside the cathedral. In 1989 he led the company on a debut tour of the Soviet Union that included performances at the Bol'shoy Theater, highlighted by a 30-minute backstage conversation with then President Mikhail Gorbachev and his wife, Raisa. Muti has been an annual guest at the Salzburg Festival for more than twenty years, and led The Philadelphia Orchestra in its debut there in 1987. He is a regular guest with the Berlin Philharmonic and Vienna Philharmonic orchestras.

Maestro Muti lives in Ravenna with his wife, Cristina, and their three children. He is a Cavaliere di Gran Croce of the Italian Republic, an Honorary Ambassador to the United Nations High

Dear Maestro Muti,

It is with great pleasure that I join your many friends around the world in congratulating you on the anniversary of your twenty years with The Philadelphia Orchestra. ❧ *On the occasion of this celebration, it is appropriate to applaud not only your exceptional contribution to music, but most particularly your commitment to the refugee cause.* ❧ *Your humanitarian endeavors as UNHCR's Honorary Ambassador are deeply appreciated. By lending your name and your talent in support of the world's 17 million refugees, you help us assure that their plight is not forgotten.* ❧ *Thank you for joining forces with us to assist our constant endeavor to defend the rights of refugees and to promote world peace.*

SADAKO OGATA

The High Commissioner For Refugees, United Nations

Commissioner for Refugees, and an honorary member of the Royal Academy of Music (London), the Accademia di Santa Cecilia (Rome), and the Accademia Luigi Cherubini (Florence), as well as holding honorary doctorates from the University of Bologna, the University of Pennsylvania, and several other universities. He has been awarded the Verdienstkreuz of the Federal Republic of Germany and the 1989 Pennsylvania Governor's Award for Excellence in the Arts. After relinquishing his post as Music Director of The Philadelphia Orchestra at the end of this season, Maestro Muti will assume the title of Laureate Conductor.

BERNARD JACOBSON *is the former Philadelphia Orchestra Program Annotator and Musicologist. He is currently Artistic Director of the Residentie Orkest in The Hague*

A MAN OF ESSENCES

by Matthew Gurewitsch

When an artist holds a place of established eminence, his achievements may come to be taken for granted. Thus, when Riccardo Muti led the orchestra and chorus of La Scala in the Mozart Requiem on the 200th anniversary of the composer's death last December, one critic in Milan noted the maestro's "nth roaring success:" casual praise, surely, for a performance as extraordinary in its dramatic ardor as in the lyric refinement of its details, polished (as the critic well knew) in an exacting public rehearsal that very morning.

If the aquiline Muti profile and ebony mane seem an icon now, as distant from real life as if struck in a medal, perhaps a look into the past will restore him to the third dimension. Back in a dusty file, there is an indignant editorial by a leading columnist (since deceased), published in September 1979, in response to Muti's appointment as Music Director of The Philadelphia Orchestra. Deep down, he wanted the post to go to an American, though citizenship was not quite a requirement. He would have countenanced the choice of — well, let us observe discretion (the three non-American conductors he mentioned are all enjoying significant international careers). But as for Muti, no.

Time has more than justified Muti's election. Maybe it is a little harder in Philadelphia than elsewhere to realize how much more: in

the handsome spaces of the Academy of Music, a core of symphonic sound carries from the stage to the hall, but not its finest sheen. Still, even here, Muti and The Philadelphia Orchestra have made blissful music: in Mendelssohn's overture *Meeresstille und glückliche Fahrt* earlier this season, for instance, with its shimmering palette and sweeping joy at the close, or in the *Rückertlieder* of Mahler, buzzing and sunny as Frederica von Stade sang of the busyness of honeybees at work in the secrecy of their hive. But to hear the maestro and his players set Carnegie Hall ringing with Elgar's *In the South* or Tchaikovsky's Symphony No. 4 last season was to witness sonic splendor of another order.

These readings of Muti's and countless more bespeak a musical mind in which an abundance of gifts, each rare, are balanced in still rarer harmony: against the exquisite sense of color, timbre, and texture, the rigorous attention to architecture; against the noble seriousness, the fantasy and elegance; against the unfailing classical poise, the rapture.

A dozen years ago, the flowering of Muti's art that Philadelphia has had the great good fortune to witness could no more have been foreseen with perfect accuracy than any other future development. Still, there were powerful indications: his comet-like emergence at the Guido Cantelli International Conductors' Competition in 1967; his early collaborations with the Soviet titan of the keyboard

Sviatoslav Richter at the Florence Maggio Musicale in 1968; his inspired and inspirational leadership of that festival beginning in 1969; his selection as successor to the crusty eminence Otto Klemperer at the Philharmonia Orchestra in London in 1973, ushering the players from exhaustion to brilliant vitality.

There are stories from Muti's younger days that bear repeating, and others that scarcely have been told. That he found his calling (or rather that his calling found him) one day when a student orchestra at the Naples Conservatory suddenly lost its conductor is well known. Less familiar is the background to his prize-winning appearance at the Cantelli in Milan. The contestants' task at each stage was to perform, after only an hour's rehearsal, a selection from a prescribed list of works they had had several months to study and prepare (that year, Beethoven's Symphony No. 7, Brahms's Symphony No. 4, the Overture to Verdi's *I vespri siciliani*, and Stravinsky's *Jeu de cartes*).

As a student at the Milan Conservatory, Muti had come to the attention of a baroness, a patroness of the arts and president of a society called Gioventù Musicale Italiana. His potential was evident to her, and when the time came for him to prepare for his big chance, she hired an orchestra in Prague, where for a week the fledgling maestro rehearsed Dvořák's *New World* Symphony, Tchaikovsky's Symphony No. 5, the Brahms Alto Rhapsody, and by Beethoven the Symphony No. 7, the *Leonore* Overture No. 3, and the Prisoners' Chorus from *Fidelio*. Then they all toured Northern

Italy together, also at the baroness's expense, for nearly two weeks, passing through the provinces and finally—the Big Time, as it seemed—to Bergamo. As the Cantelli jury confirmed, her faith had not been misplaced. Muti had an advantage not given to many, yes; but then, he did his part.

His first encounter with Richter was auspicious too. The pianist had signed on for a concert at the Maggio Musicale under a renowned conductor who had suddenly become ill. Muti was standing by. Would Richter play with this unknown youngster?, the management inquired. If he is a good musician, Richter replied, I will. Muti was brought to meet him, they went through the score together, Richter declared himself pleased, and the performance went forward; a signal success, and another milestone in what was shaping up as a charmed career.

At the Maggio Musicale, Muti won new audiences to neglected romantic grand operas (Rossini's *Guillaume Tell*, Meyerbeer's *L'Africaine*, Spontini's *Agnes von Hohenstaufen*), as well as symphonic repertoire both classic and contemporary. The excitement kept the young firebrand in the news; and then there was news of a more tempestuous sort in 1973, when Muti was engaged for the first time to conduct an opera at La Scala. At the dress rehearsal of *I Puritani*, the maestro's exasperation with the whims of a certain star singer mounted to such a pitch that he threw down his baton, climbed into his Fiat, and roared straight down the highway to his home in Marina di Ravenna. Well, those fences have been mended. But as the record shows, Muti was not only a golden boy; he was also a hothead for art, for principle.

By 1979, of course, The Philadelphia Orchestra had no need to receive its estimation of Muti from the foreign press. The players knew him well. They had made their first acquaintance in 1972. In 1977, the relationship was formalized with Muti's appointment as Principal Guest Conductor. By the time he was named Music Director, the Orchestra was as much the captive of its history as it was the custodian. A visionary was needed, and happily, a visionary was at hand.

A visionary, it should be said, of a most scrupulous kind. For all his personal magnetism, and without any false modesty, he came to Philadelphia as the servant of music. Some conductors, among them such legendary ones as Leonard Bernstein and Sergiu Celibidache, have made remarks to the effect that in a truly great performance they feel as if they themselves had written the scores, or were even creating them on the spot. Watching Muti on the podium and listening to his players, one senses no such imperializing by the performer, no such annihilation of the composer, nor would Muti desire it. "Even in scores that have become part of me," he said recently, "I always feel that I am evoking something that has been said to me so that I may say it to others. I bear the word of another and bring it to the listeners as a message. I give what is passing through me."

He is no empire-builder. In the sense that he believes the messages in music are meant for all who will open their ears to hear them, he is supremely egalitarian. In the sense that he accepts no artistic compromise, he is an elitist. As he remarked to an interviewer on student radio at the very beginning, if the Philadelphia audience was not receptive to his ideas, he would be content to go home to Ravenna and lead a civic orchestra there. Disbelieve if you will; he must have meant it.

Asked to put those ideas into words, Muti said not long ago, "I would like people to understand the meaning of a musical performance: to listen to music as a gift, and to take part in a concert or an opera as a rite in which the celebrants are not only the musicians but also the public, reaching out in a cultural and spiritual experience that is all-embracing."

And that is what his record has told us. Looking back over the accomplishments of the Muti era, we find in the music conviction and high purpose, securely beyond the tides of fashion. In a city without other world-class orchestral ensembles and not much visited by touring star orchestras from all over the globe, Muti recognized that the Orchestra must bear the torch for the entire symphonic literature. The Philadelphia Orchestra could not serve its city by specializing: it could not be a Beethoven orchestra without being a Berlioz orchestra, too, a Mozart orchestra and a Mendelssohn orchestra and a Mahler orchestra, a Schubert orchestra, a Tchaikovsky orchestra, not to mention an orchestra for Shulamit Ran, Richard Wernick, and Bernard Rands.

Muti tuned The Philadelphia Orchestra to meet all these challenges and more. Recall his systematic explorations of Prokofiev and Scriabin, or his excursions into so curious a character as Ferruccio Busoni, represented by a kaleidoscopic suite from his opera *Turandot*, where ribbons of romance chase shards of the grotesque. Or think of his operas in concert: invitations into a mesmerizing theater of the mind, supreme illustrations of the drama that lives in Gluck's, Verdi's, Wagner's, Puccini's words and music, self-sufficient, independent of the trappings of the stage.

It is Muti's genius to focus on essences. He is no showman in the line of Stokowski, who would drum up business for The Philadelphia Orchestra with lunchtime potpourris for the shoppers in the atrium of Wanamaker's. Some observers have grumbled at Muti's reserve. They wish he did the social circuit (he prefers to keep to his personal circle); that he would sometimes lighten up with some pops (even at a party, he plays real music); that he would smile for the camera (he is more apt to scowl).

In the age of personality, Muti chooses to let his work speak for him. Through it, perhaps paradoxically, perhaps not, he stands before the public completely revealed, not as he might be through trivial anecdote, but in the truth of his character. And what shines forth is a splendid intelligence untrammeled by ego, hungry for understanding, confident in its conclusions, yet never at rest.

He speaks of his profession with a certain solemnity. "The conductor looks like he is on a pedestal, but he is not. Even if he is surrounded by the orchestra in front and the audience behind, he is lonely. He must find the source of inspiration in himself. His instrument is outside, he must bring to it his ideas. The public is the other entity to whom he must convey his vision. Especially after a performance I feel lonely. Even if there has been a big success, for me it is a moment of retrospection: why have I not achieved what I wanted to achieve? The questions start after the last chord."

What keeps him going?, I asked him once. He laughed quietly. "Interesting question," he replied. "I don't know." A long silence followed. "Certainly the world of music is like a magic garden. You want to explore more and more, knowing that you are trying to find something that you will never find."

He earns his laurels every day.

MATTHEW GUREWITSCH *has written about music and musicians for* The New York Times, The Atlantic, *and publications around the world.*

Riccardo Muti and Opera in Italy

by William Weaver

The performance of Verdi's *I masnadieri* at the Teatro Comunale in Florence during the winter of 1969–70 had little to recommend it — beyond the music of Verdi itself — and I still don't know why I bothered to go. It was a revival of a production from a Maggio Musicale festival several years earlier; I had already seen it, disliked it, and said as much in print. The staging was by Erwin Piscator, a historic figure from the pre-Hitler German theater; but his production was pretentious, clumsy, ugly. The festival cast, itself less than first rate, had now been replaced by second-string artists. The veteran conductor Gianandrea Gavazzeni had ceded the baton to a young, unknown maestro. But, after all, *I masnadieri* was not an opera often programmed, and since every note of Verdi has the power to lure me, I went.

The house was at least half empty. And such audience as there was had that listless air characteristic of a papered hall: subscribers had given their tickets to an impoverished relative, or the housekeeper, or a supposedly music-loving neighbor. I could have stretched out full-length in any row of the stalls without disturbing anyone.

No one with a functioning ear can fail to be moved by the opening bars of *I masnadieri*, however; and the brief cello concerto — which Verdi wrote for the great Alfredo Piatti to play — was instantly effective. Straining my eyes in the darkness, I managed to read in the program the name of the unknown conductor: Riccardo Muti.

The production it turned out was no better than I remembered it, but the grade B singers were inspired to give their best, and the performance caught fire. It was not, of course, spontaneous combustion. Muti transferred his own vitality and conviction into every note of the work. Within minutes, I was blind to the awful production, the awkward flights of steps that made the singers look warily at their feet, the arty stage-darkness that made the action difficult to follow.

At the end, my chief thought was to discover the next occasion to hear Muti, and it came within a few weeks (I am hazy about dates, and in any case these are impressions, not biography). Again at the Comunale, Muti conducted the Verdi Requiem: the first of many performances I was to hear under him, each infused with that special intensity Verdi seems to inspire in this interpreter. Muti's readings of the Mass are never, to use the tired cliché, operatic; but they are dramatic on a larger-than-life scale. They are, literally, a matter of life and death.

The Florence *Masnadieri* was not to be the last absurd production I was to see with Muti conducting. Some of Luca Ronconi's worst excesses at La Scala — Mirella Freni carried on a wobbling platform like a Madonna in an Easter procession (*Ernani*), Chris Merritt expressing his inability to enter a house when, in fact, he has just emerged from it (*Guillaume Tell*) — were compensated for by Muti's profound penetration of the score.

Maestro Muti and La Scala: it would be more correct to say that Maestro Muti is La Scala. He is its personification, its soul and its pride. ❧ Muti has dedicated himself to ensuring that La Scala has come to symbolize "the world's most famous opera house": the one that people think of first when music is mentioned at its highest levels. ❧ Maestro Muti and The Philadelphia Orchestra: here, too, one might refer to a form of symbiosis between Muti himself and the American institution. He has raised the Orchestra to highest professional and qualitative standards, opened up new horizons, filling it with life, and making it unquestionably one of the best orchestras in the world. ❧ La Scala and the Philadelphia, enriched by his contribution, his severity, his moral tension, have provided Muti with fertile ground to sow and harvest his gifts as a conductor. One of the most powerful is his instinct for cultural syncretism: purity of sound harnessed simultaneously to a profound sense of musical drama. The evidence is there in the Philadelphia, not just in its symphonic recordings but its operatic works, whilst La Scala's orchestra has finally mastered a major symphonic repertoire, an unusual achievement for Italy. It is now capable of playing Beethoven with a confidence possessed by no other orchestra in the country. ❧ Now Maestro Muti is leaving The Philadelphia Orchestra: a painful decision, unquestionably, dictated by purely personal reasons, but one that must be interpreted in the light of uncompromising and utterly honest spirit that has inspired all his decisions. ❧ A difficult choice but one that most certainly reflects his deepest convictions.

CARLO FONTANA
Sovrintendente, Teatro alla Scala

Though some of my happiest memories of Muti's conducting are associated with Verdi, his operatic repertory has developed rapidly and ranges widely. The above-mentioned Scala *Tell*, given virtually in its sublimely long entirety, was a high point (though a previous performance of the same opera in Florence was perhaps even more enjoyable, thanks to a more sensible staging and perhaps a superior cast). Muti's Mozart — which I heard first in Florence, then at La Scala, then on records — has become widely familiar to European audiences. And, just recently, he inaugurated the Scala season with *Parsifal*, a bold step, not only because he was breaking an unwritten, but firm rule at the great Milan house: that the opening work of the season should be Italian, preferably by Verdi. The immense success of this brave venture opens new vistas, perhaps even of a Muti *Ring* (for decades Wagner has largely been entrusted, at La Scala, to conductors imported from the north).

Muti's perceptive exploration of the repertory has led him even to produce and conduct Pergolesi's *Lo frate'nnamorato* at La Scala, though the work would, at first sight, hardly have seemed ideal in dimension or in style to the house (it is hard to conceive of a Milanese audience laughing at Neapolitan jokes); but the performance was a success. Moving into a different area of operatic history, Muti has also revived Cherubini's *Lodoïska*, which had been absent from La Scala for about forty years (and had been less than a triumph at the last revival). Muti's persuasive recordings of Cherubini's Masses had prepared his admirers for a keen and sensitively shaped presentation of the music, yet few, perhaps, were prepared for the splendor of the work itself, which Muti revealed without the help of a star-studded cast, but with a carefully selected and a patiently trained team of singing artists.

Defined as a "comédie héroique," *Lodoïska* is a difficult work for the contemporary audience, which likes operas to fit squarely into one of two categories: serious or comic. The public wants to laugh or cry. But Cherubini's "rescue" tale, with its suggestion of violence and torment, its deprival of freedom, its divided loves, ends happily; so some spectators feel cheated of the catharsis of tears. The same fate has befallen many of Rossini's semi-seria operas, and having reestablished the performability of *Guillaume Tell*, perhaps Muti will take up newly emerging Rossini works like *La gazza ladra* and *Torvaldo e Dorliska*, which Pesaro and other, smaller Italian festivals have mounted.

While he continues to conduct (and record) Verdi and Mozart and, now, Wagner, Muti is clearly still eager to extend his own range and, at the same time, expand the receptivity of the Scala audience, notoriously resistant to new ideas. As warehouses full of used-once scenery are there to prove, the mere revival of an unknown work does not guarantee comprehension, still less renewed popularity. But Muti often gives works the kiss of life. Many years ago, I remember, I heard at Maggio Musicale a distinguished senior conductor lead a somnambulistic performance of a Spontini rarity; *Agnes von Hohenstaufen*: it seemed monumental, endless, and irredeemably dull. Some years later, still quite early in his career, Muti conducted a radio performance, and, for professional reasons, I had to tape it. I had actually planned a dinner party on my terrace for the evening, so I kept the radio's volume almost inaudibly low to allow my guests and me to talk (I was planning to study the tape the next day, in solitude). But the guests, opera lovers all, kept shushing one another, until I finally turned up the volume and we listened seriously to the opera, eating in silence broken only by the gurgle of wine being poured or the inadvertent scrape of a spoon. The performance was electrifying; the opera I had once scorned now seemed a vital, irresistible masterpiece.

A few years ago, the Rome Opera revived the work and I rushed to hear it. But the spark was missing, and Spontini's *Agnes* seemed as dead (if not buried) as her historical counterpart.

Muti has a house near Ravenna (where his wife grew up), and spends as much time there as he can steal from his crammed schedule. Two years ago, Cristina Muti became Honorary President of the Ravenna Festival, which — under her guidance (and with her husband's regular presence) — has taken a new and adventurous turn. There is talk of a collaboration with the Rossini Opera Festival in Pesaro, farther down the Adriatic coast. Muti's sense of adventure will have a new area in which to achieve favorite projects.

William Weaver, *translator and music critic, lives in Italy where he serves as arts correspondent for the* Financial Times *of London and contributes to other international publications.*

WITH THE LATE CARL ORFF, AFTER
A PERFORMANCE OF HIS *CARMINA
BURANA* IN BERLIN, 1980

Riccardo Muti
mit besonderem Dank und in
Bewunderung für seine gleichsam
zweite Uraufführung
der Carmina Burana
mit den Berliner Philharmonikern
am 23. VI. 1980
herzlichst

Carl Orff

Riccardo Muti and Central Europe: Salzburg, Berlin, Vienna

by Derek Weber

For any young conductor the entry in the exclusive Central European cultural triangle formed by Salzburg, Berlin, and Vienna is an extremely difficult venture. When Riccardo Muti was invited to the Salzburg Festival for the first time, in 1971, he was only thirty. The kingdom of Mozart (and Richard Strauss) was in the hands of the aged Karl Böhm then, whereas Herbert von Karajan was the unchallenged master of the Festival.

At that time Karajan was in favour of the idea of bringing in a fresh breeze by adding some Italian spirit, inviting artists like the Milanese stage director Giorgio Strehler and extending the range of the Italian repertory in general. Riccardo Muti was chosen as a conductor at home in the realm of bel canto and able to supervise the new staging of Gaetano Donizetti's *Don Pasquale*. Although the production as a whole was not really appreciated by the critics, the press for Muti himself was excellent. The prominent Bavarian newspaper *Süddeutsche Zeitung*, for instance, called him "the disclosure of the evening."

Muti's debut in Salzburg had consequences: During the following years he was given the opportunity to conduct Festival concerts with the Vienna Philharmonic, the first of which contained Rossini's *Semiramide* Overture, Schumann's Piano Concerto (with Svi- atoslav Richter as soloist) and the Cherubini Requiem. In 1975 Muti gave his first Philharmonic concert in Vienna (within a cycle dedicated to the *Jeunesse musicale*) and was invited to lead the Philharmonic's Japan tour that same year.

Already two years earlier, in February 1973, he had given his debut at the Vienna State Opera, conducting the first night of a new *Aida* production. As in 1971 in Salzburg, the Viennese critics pulled to pieces scenery, direction, and most of the singers, but lauded Muti. The next productions at the State Opera were Giuseppe Verdi's *La forza del destino* (1974), Bellini's *Norma,* (1977) and, the temporarily last one so far, *Rigoletto* in Verdi's original version. With the purified *Norma* Muti had to fight the resistance of some singers only; the attempt to restore Verdi's score called up the belligerent minority of the friends of the high C who booed down the singers as well as the conductor.

One year after his Salzburg *Don Pasquale,* Riccardo Muti gave his first concert with the Berlin Philharmonic, in Berlin on June 15, 1972. The program of this performance (and many others to follow) was more unorthodox than those usually designed for the more conservative audiences in Salzburg and Vienna. It contained Béla Bartók's Second Piano Concerto (soloist: Maurizio Pollini) and Sergei Prokofiev's rarely performed Third Symphony.

23

The time lag in modernity can clearly be understood also by the fact that Carl Orff's *Carmina Burana* saw a triumphant performance in Berlin in 1980. (At the same time, this concert was one of the exceptional occasions when the aged composer left his Bavarian home to join the audience, and he wrote this about the performance: "Riccardo Muti — With special thanks and admiration for his 'second world premiere,' so to speak, of *Carmina Burana* with the Berlin Philharmonic on June 23, 1980. Most cordially, Carl Orff.")

The Salzburg performance was to follow only five years later—but with the same enthusiastic response by the public as in Berlin.

There have been other memorable Muti performances in Vienna as well as Berlin and Salzburg. Two pieces which I remember very well are Joseph Haydn's *Sieben letzte Worte des Erlösers am Kreuze* (*Seven Last Words of Our Saviour on the Cross*) in Salzburg in August 1982 (given also in Berlin in 1985) and Ravel's *Boléro* in the Vienna Musikverein Hall in March 1983. Seven months before, Riccardo Muti had definitely established himself as a Mozart conductor and eventual successor of Karl Böhm (who died in 1983) with the new production of *Così fan tutte*, which was to remain in the repertory of the Salzburg Festival until the Mozart anniversary of 1991.

From 1972 to 1991 Riccardo Muti has conducted more than forty programs with the Vienna Philharmonic and more than thirty with the Berlin Philharmonic. His soloist partners included Claudio Arrau, Emil Gilels, Murray Perahia, Gidon Kremer, and others. He gave one concert—the first he did in Vienna, in October 1974—with the Vienna Symphony Orchestra; in 1976 he appeared with the Philharmonia Orchestra of London and later — of course — with "his" Philadelphia Orchestra.

Together with a small number of other conductors, Riccardo Muti today forms an indispensable part of Central European musical life. In particular, the cooperation with the Vienna Philharmonic seems to have become closer than ever. He is one of the few persons who have been awarded the *Ehrenring* ("Ring of Honor") of the orchestra as a visible sign of high esteem. The ceremony took place before a Salzburg rehearsal last year, on the 26th of July, just before his 50th birthday.

The result of his Central European activities can easily be examined by various recordings, such as Mozart's three da Ponte operas and Schubert's symphonies (with the Vienna Philharmonic), and some works of Handel, Mozart, Bruckner, and Richard Strauss (with the Berlin Philharmonic). Muti still has many projects here, ranging from a new production of *La clemenza di Tito* at the Salzburg Festival (1992) and a revival of *Le nozze di Figaro* at the Vienna State Opera in 1993, to some ventures of a long-term nature, like the recording of all Mozart symphonies with the Vienna Philharmonic. Whereas Philadelphia has to confront a loss, Central Europe is hoping to encounter Riccardo Muti at least a little bit more often than during the last decades.

DEREK WEBER *is the music critic of the* Salzburger Nachrichten.

MUTI IN THE RECORDING STUDIO

by Daniel Webster

IN THE CONTROL ROOM
DURING A RECORDING SESSION
IN MEMORIAL HALL, 1985

Riccardo Muti's appointment as Music Director of The Philadelphia Orchestra came the day of the Three Mile Island accident in 1979, and many felt he was stepping into a recording scene almost as rich in disaster potential as the events at the nuclear power plant.

The major U.S. recording companies had been made almost irrelevant by firms able to take advantage of lower costs in Europe. And Philadelphia, which had become the most-recorded American orchestra in the 1960s and early 1970s, was recording less and less.

But Muti had in his luggage an exclusive contract with EMI. The British firm was committed to expanding its presence in the United States, Japan, and Europe with Muti and the Philadelphians. Muti was already EMI's star in Britain, where he had guided the Philharmonia since 1978, and had recorded substantial symphonic and operatic repertoire with that London orchestra.

Muti and the Philadelphians found other directions on the way to creating a weighty catalogue that ranges from the contemporary to the 18th century, but with an emphasis on the 19th-century giants. Their work together has taken them through the end of the analog and the digital eras of LP records into the era of the compact disc.

Muti's interest in Russian music is plain from his Philadelphia recordings. Among his earliest LP's were Prokofiev's *Romeo and Juliet*, Stravinsky's great ballets *Le Sacre du printemps* and *L'Oiseau de feu*, and *Petrouchka*, (the latter of which won Germany's Deutscher Schallplatten award for Best Symphonic Recording) Rimsky-Korsakov's *Scheherezade*, and Tchaikovsky's *Serenade for Strings* and *1812*

Overture. Many of the Russian works Muti programmed early in his Philadelphia tenure — Tchaikovsky's Symphonies Nos. 1 through 6, *Manfred*, Piano Concerto No. 1, and Prokofiev's *Ivan the Terrible* — he already had recorded with the Philharmonia.

Other early recordings, in the French tradition, included Franck's Symphony in D minor and *Le Chausseur maudit*, Liszt's *Faust* Symphony and *Les Préludes* (which won the Grand Prix from the Franz Liszt Society in Budapest), Ravel's *Symphonie Espagnole* with Falla's *Three-Cornered Hat,* and Berlioz's *Roméo et Juliette.*

The Academy of Music's dry acoustics and periodic subway rumble have made it generally unusable for recording. Since Muti became Music Director, the Orchestra has recorded, sometimes with snow sifting down through the roof, in the old Metropolitan Opera House on North Broad Street, and then on a basketball court at Memorial Hall, more than 110 years old, in Fairmount Park. The heating system in the hall is so loud that it must be shut off during takes. And because recording is done during the fall, winter, and early spring, records are made there by musicians bundled in sweaters, scarves, and hats. Nonetheless, the first issue of that effort, Mahler's Symphony No. 1, received several international honors. Another project that received notice was the complete Scriabin symphonies, a rarity in the entire recording catalogue. Perhaps the culmination of the EMI/Muti/Philadelphia collaboration was the release of the complete Beethoven symphonies, Muti's first, and the first recorded by an American orchestra for compact disc.

In the 1980s Muti ended the exclusive aspect of his relationship with EMI, and the Dutch-headquartered Philips label contracted for

some recordings with him in Philadelphia, beginning with the complete Brahms symphonies and continuing with the almost-completed Prokofiev symphonies. A recording of Orff's choral work *Carmina Burana* is planned for some time in 1993. In order to make Puccini's *Tosca*, the first Muti/Philadelphia recording of opera, their technicians returned to the Academy of Music with a new approach. German engineer Volker Strauss put 55 microphones onstage, ignoring the quality of the hall by taking sound directly from instruments and singers. Once complete, the tape will be played back for final recording in a resonant church in Holland, and the resulting disc will sound as if the performance was captured in a rich acoustical ambience. Philips also used this approach to record Leoncavallo's *Pagliacci* in Philadelphia this spring.

A memorial tribute to Philadelphia composer Vincent Persichetti on New World Records paired his Symphony No. 5 conducted by Muti with the Piano Concerto conducted by Charles Dutoit.

Another, to feature the music of Composer-in-Residence Bernard Rands, is awaiting completion.

Apart from Philadelphia, Muti is under long-term contract to record Verdi operas at La Scala for EMI, and Philips began projects with Muti at La Scala with Rossini's *Guillaume Tell* in 1989. Sony signed Muti for Cherubini's rarely performed opera *Lodoïska*, which he conducted at La Scala in 1991, and more will certainly follow.

EMI also regularly records Muti's work with the Berlin and Vienna Philharmonics, including a complete cycle of Schubert symphonies with Vienna, and his productions of Mozart operas at the Salzburg Festival. Future releases include the complete Schumann symphonies with Vienna, and Haydn's *Seven Last Words of Our Saviour on the Cross*, recorded in 1991 with the Berlin Philharmonic.

DANIEL WEBSTER *is the senior music critic of* The Philadelphia Inquirer.

THE
PHILADELPHIA
SEASON

❧

One could discern an artistic direction, if one were looking, from Riccardo Muti's early concerts as a young guest conductor in the 1970s. Indeed, his very first two programs, in 1972, introduced works that previously had not been played by the Orchestra. The first was a Mozart Piano Concerto, K. 271 in E flat major, and the second was *Appunti per un Credo*, a 1962 work by Italian composer Giorgio Ghedini.

This pattern was to become the backbone of his artistic mission in Philadelphia: to expose the Orchestra and its subscription audience to the entire range of repertoire, with particular emphasis on works that had not been heard at those concerts, ranging from the Classical and Baroque periods of composition to world premieres of music completed only months before.

Muti's goal, he often said, was to make the Orchestra "a more perfect instrument, technically and culturally," and to do this he sought to provide new, ever more challenging musical opportunities. Through the performance of concert opera, he explains, "the orchestra learns to be more flexible, to sing with the singers, to play with more imagination than in purely symphonic music." Through the performance of chamber music, players refresh themselves artistically and personally. Through the commissioning and performance of new works, particularly from American composers, the organization sharpens its awareness of, and participation in, the culture of today.

During Riccardo Muti's tenure, 44 new musicians were hired. Muti was so careful to find the right player that sometimes no one was chosen from the first round of auditions, so others had to be arranged. He also encouraged more Orchestra members to perform as soloists, providing yet another stimulus for growth.

Maestro Muti's insistence on the highest standards extended to every aspect of his work with the Orchestra. Players soon learned that each piece of music was to be treated as sacrosanct, with no cuts, excerpts, or changes allowed. Mistakes in the printed parts were ferreted out immediately, and corrected. It became a mission of the Orchestra's music librarians to seek out and correct the parts in advance in order to save rehearsal time. Other orchestras around the world soon began turning to Philadelphia for the accurate versions. The concern for fidelity extended to the program books, in which titles of works came to be printed in the language in which they were written.

And like Leopold Stokowski many years earlier, Muti demanded that the audience show equal respect for the music. Subscribers soon learned that they had better be in their seats by 7:59, because once the music began, at 8:00 sharp, they would not be seated until the end of the first piece. By deliberately including, or sometimes even concluding a concert, with a quiet, introverted work, such as Haydn's *Seven Last Words of Our Saviour on the Cross,* he asked peo-

1980-1981 SEASON
START OF A NEW ERA
RICCARDO MUTI
MUSIC DIRECTOR

PHILADELPHIA
FEB 11 '81
PA.

U.S. POSTAGE
1 86

P.B. METER
637890

ple to open themselves to a different level of experiencing music. "The public will respond if you show them the way," he said. He was proven right, and in the process, the Orchestra's subscription base rose from 27,000 people in Muti's first season as Music Director, to over 35,000 during his last.

In order to best serve the growing audience, and particularly to meet the needs of the young people he wished to introduce to the Orchestra, Muti cut out performances in Wilmington and Baltimore, decreased the number in Washington, D.C., and added new Philadelphia series on Monday, Tuesday, Thursday, and Friday evenings. After being virtually sold out in advance during his first seasons, the Orchestra intentionally capped subscription sales at 90%, thus leaving more single tickets available for new listeners.

As these new listeners join the audience, Riccardo Muti leaves the Orchestra with a public that has come to expect innovation as well as tradition, vocal music as well as instrumental music, soft endings as well as dramatically loud ones. He leaves, as he arrived, with the challenge to strive for the best, because in music, as he says, "there is never the word 'end' to what you have to achieve."

We needed someone who could bring us the cross-pollenation of broader cultural experiences. ❧ We needed a conductor with the willingness to take risks and the youthful energy to suffer the consequences. ❧ We needed someone who could demystify music and the Orchestra so we could perceive it not as a frozen relic of a romantic past but as a continuing intellectual process engaged in by thinking individuals. ❧ We needed someone who cared enough and was passionate enough to yell at us once in a while. ❧ And we needed someone who, instead of settling in to a comfortable lifetime job, would give us the best, highly-intense years of his life and then move on. ❧ You filled all these particulars beyond my wildest dreams.
DAN ROTTENBERG, *from a column entitled "Dear Riccardo Muti,"* Welcomat, *February 5, 1992*

Riccardo Muti knows, better than anyone else I've met, what makes human beings tick. There, in a sense, you have the vital clue to his gifts, because such insight is both a personal quality and, for a conductor, a technical one. To be a great conductor, among other things, you have to be able to get inside players' and singers' minds (as well as composers' and listeners' minds). Imagine a front-desk player in The Philadelphia Orchestra who, with a concerto date looming three months in the

PERMANENT MEMBERS OF THE ORCHESTRA ENGAGED BY RICCARDO MUTI

1979–80
Kathryn Picht, cello
Patricia Weimer Hess, cello

1980–81
Cynthia Williams, violin

1981–82
Kazuo Tokito, piccolo
Philip Kates, violin
Charles Vernon, trombone
Patrick Connolly, viola
Joseph Alessi, trombone
David Cramer, flute

1982–83
Barbara Govatos, violin
Mark Gigliotti, bassoon
John Hood, bass

1983–84
Judy Geist, viola
Paul Arnold, violin
Nancy Bean, violin
Richard Ranti, bassoon

1984–85
Yumi Ninomiya Scott, violin
Laura Park, violin
Dmitri Levin, violin
Luis Biava, violin
David Fay, bass
Christian Euler, viola

1985–86
Boris Balter, violin
Robert Cafaro, cello

1986–87
Eric Carlson, trombone
Jonathan Blumenfeld, oboe
Blair Bollinger, bass trombone
Duane Rosengard, bass

1987–88
Ohad Bar-David, cello
Robert Kesselman, bass

1988–89
Sang-Min Park, cello

1989–90
Cynthia Koledo
 DeAlmeida, oboe
Jeffry Kirschen, horn
Don S. Liuzzi, timpani
Calvin C. Price, trumpet

1990–91
Jeffrey Khaner, flute
John Koen, cello
Hirono Oka, violin
Peter Stumpf, cello

1991–92
Robert W. Earley, trumpet
Kimberly Fisher, violin
Michael Ludwig, violin
Paul Roby, violin
Peter Smith, oboe

future, is racking his brain for a way to ask the Music Director if he could possibly take a couple of days off playing the demanding adjacent program. Then he gets a call from the Orchestra office: Muti, away in Milan where he is busy preparing for the opening of another La Scala season, has himself telephoned Philadelphia to suggest that the player in question might like to do exactly that. It is this kind of understanding, of empathy, that repeatedly takes the breath away. The same character-istic told Muti, taking over an orchestra whose players had for years been discouraged from playing chamber music, that chamber music was just what the players needed to revitalize their own deep response to music; it prompted him to call for the official institution of the chamber series that is now an integral part of the Philadelphia Orchestra season, and to keep a close eye on its planning and implementation. ❧ Such qualities are the source of deep satisfactions. For me as program annota-tor and musicologist there have been many other such pleasures on a more specific plane: his demand that the program notes match as far as possible the cultural stance of the Orchestra, and incidentally that they should contain music examples whenever appropriate; his respect at the same time for the professionalism of his staff, so that a nervous inquiry whether he might want to see my very first set of Philadelphia notes in advance was met by a smiling assurance that he would be happy to read them on the evening of the concert; his unfailing fidelity to the spirit and style of every composer he conducted, which made it unnecessary ever to call and ask, "Are you using the new critical revised edition?," or "Are you taking such-and-such a repeat?," or "Are you going back to the original scoring?," or "Are you playing it uncut?" — I simply knew that he would be; the equally unquenchable intellectual curiosity that made him receptive to my intimations of the latest musicological discoveries, whether about the preferable version of a Mozart sinfonia concertante, or about Beethoven's previously unsuspected desire to have the violins muted in the slow movement of the Pastorale *Symphony; his insistence that music is a going concern, not just a museum, and that performing and commissioning new works is a prerequisite for keeping an orchestra fresh; his realization that music is also a part of a broader life and a broader culture, embracing all the arts, and embracing philosophy and science and the betterment of society too. ❧ All this made my work here an annotator's and musicologist's dream. Am I forgetting the other fun-damental thing—the sheer greatness of the performances? I could never forget it, or him.*

BERNARD JACOBSON, *Former Philadelphia Orchestra Program Annotator and Musicologist, Artistic Director of the Residentie Orkest in The Hague*

Works Given First Philadelphia Orchestra Performances Conducted by Riccardo Muti

1972–73

MOZART Piano Concerto No. 9, K. 271: Philippe Entremont (Philadelphia, New York)

GHEDINI *Appunti per un Credo*

1973–74

BERLIOZ *Waverley* Overture

BUSONI Suite from *Turandot*

1974–75

VIVALDI Concerto in A major for Strings & Continuo

PROKOFIEV Sinfonietta (Philadelphia, Baltimore, Washington, D.C.)

BRUCKNER Symphony No. 6 (Philadelphia, New York)

1975–76

ROTA *Variazioni sopra una tema gioviale* (Philadelphia, New York)

1976–77

MOZART Symphony No. 25, K. 183 (Philadelphia, New York)

1977–78

PENDERECKI Symphony No. 1

PETRASSI *Coro di morti*: Philadelphia College of the Performing Arts Chorus

VIVALDI Concerto in C major, *La solennità di San Lorenzo*: Norman Carol, William de Pasquale, William Stokking

PROKOFIEV *Ivan the Terrible*: Mendelssohn Club (Philadelphia, New York)

1978–79

LIGETI *Ramifications* (Philadelphia, Wilmington, Washington, D.C.)

VIVALDI Flute Concerto in G minor, *La Notte*, Op. 10 No. 2: Murray Panitz

1979–80

STRAVINSKY *Orpheus* (Philadelphia, New York)

LUTOSLAWSKI Funeral Music (Philadelphia, Washington, D.C.)

1980–81

SCRIABIN Symphony No. 1: Beverly Wolff and Jon Fredric West, Mendelssohn Club (Philadelphia, New York)

ELGAR *In the South* (Philadelphia, Washington, D.C.)

SCHUMANN Overture to *Hermann und Dorothea*

1981–82

CHERUBINI Requiem in C minor: Mendelssohn Club

HAYDN *Seven Last Words of Our Saviour on the Cross* (Philadelphia, Wilmington, Washington, D.C.)

STRAVINSKY *Apollo* (Philadelphia, Washington, D.C.)

BLOCH Violin Concerto: Yehudi Menuhin (Philadelphia, New York)

BERLIOZ *Les Nuits d'été*: Frederica von Stade

PENDERECKI Adagietto from *Paradise Lost* (Philadelphia, New York)

1982–83

BERLIOZ *Roméo et Juliette* (complete): Beverly Wolff, Philip Creech, Simon Estes, Singing City Choir

BEETHOVEN Romance No. 1: Norman Carol

DONIZETTI Overture to *Don Pasquale*

VERDI Overture to *La battaglia di Legnano*

LADERMAN Concerto for Flute, Bassoon, and Orchestra, world premiere: Murray Panitz, Bernard Garfield; commissioned by The Philadelphia Orchestra in connection with the 300th anniversary of the City of Philadelphia (Philadelphia, Washington, D.C.)

1983–84

CHERUBINI Symphony in D major

MADERNA *Music of Gaiety*: Norman Carol, Richard Woodhams (Philadelphia, Washington, D.C.)

PENDERECKI *The Dream of Jacob*, in honor of the composer's 50th birthday (Philadelphia, Washington, D.C.)

VERDI *Macbeth*, U.S. premiere of critical edition: Renato Bruson, Elizabeth Connell, Simon Estes, Westminster Symphonic Choir (Philadelphia, New York)

MOZART Ballet Music from *Idomeneo*

SCHULLER Symphony for Brass and Percussion (Philadelphia, New York)

BERLIOZ *La Mort de Cléopâtre*: Jessye Norman (Philadelphia, New York)

VIVALDI Concerto in F major for Flute, Oboe, Bassoon, Strings and Continuo, *La tempesta di mare*: Murray Panitz, Richard Woodhams, Bernard Garfield

1984–85

GLUCK *Orfeo ed Euridice* (original 1762 version): Agnes Baltsa, Margaret Marshall, Arleen Auger, Westminster Choir (Philadelphia, New York)

SALIERI *La follia di Spagna*, U.S. premiere (Philadelphia, New York)

DE ANGELIS Suite of 16th-century Lute Music for Harp and Chamber Orchestra: Marilyn Costello

VERDI Overture to *Luisa Miller* (Philadelphia, Washington, D.C.)

IRVING FINE *Notturno* for Strings and Harp: Marilyn Costello

PREMRU Music for Three Trombones, Tuba, and Orchestra, world premiere: Glenn Dodson, L. David Read, Charles Vernon, Paul Krzywicki; commissioned by the West Philadelphia Committee for The Philadelphia Orchestra (Philadelphia, New York)

1985–86

HAYDN Symphony No. 48, *Maria Theresia* (Philadelphia, Washington, D.C.)

VERDI *Rigoletto*, U.S. premiere of critical edition: Renato Bruson, Cecilia Gasdia, Michael Myers, Westminster Choir (Philadelphia, New York)

GINASTERA Cello Concerto No. 2: Aurora Natola-Ginastera

HANDEL *Water Music* (complete)

HINDEMITH Symphony in E flat major (Philadelphia, New York)

ROSSINI Sonata No. 6 in D major for Strings (Philadelphia, New York)

FAURÉ *Les Préludes de Prométhée*

DVOŘÁK Symphony No. 5 (Philadelphia, New York)

ETLER Concerto for Wind Quintet and Orchestra: Murray Panitz, Richard Woodhams, Anthony Gigliotti, Nolan Miller, Bernard Garfield (Philadelphia, New York)

WERNICK Violin Concerto, world premiere: Gregory Fulkerson (The work won the 1986 Friedheim Award.)

1986–87

ROSSINI Ballet Music from *Guillaume Tell*

RANDS *Madrigali*

BIZET *Roma* Symphony

WAGNER *Der fliegende Holländer*: Aage Haugland, Hartmut Welker, Sabine Hass, Gary Lakes, Michael Myers, Clarity James, Westminster Choir

HAYDN Symphony No. 84

CHERUBINI Overture to *Lodoïska*

CIMAROSA Overture to *L'apprensivo raggirato*

BERLIOZ *Grande symphonie funèbre et triomphale*: Choral Arts Society (Philadelphia, New York)

ROUSE *Phaethon*, world premiere; Constitutional Commission, underwritten by Johnson & Higgins (Philadelphia, New York)

SHAPEY Symphonie Concertante, world premiere; Constitutional Commission, underwritten by Johnson & Higgins (Philadelphia, New York)

1987–88

WEBER Piano Concerto No. 1: Malcolm Frager (Philadelphia, New York, Washington, D.C.)

MARTINŮ Rhapsody-Concerto for Viola and Orchestra: Joseph de Pasquale

CIMAROSA Concerto for Two Flutes and Orchestra: James Galway, Murray Panitz (Mann Music Center)

1988–89

BARTÓK Concerto for Two Pianos, Percussion, and Orchestra: Canino-Ballista Piano Duo

VERDI *Nabucco*, U.S. premiere of critical edition: Linda Roark-Strummer, Michael Myers, Paata Burchuladze, Westminster Choir (Philadelphia, New York)

DRUCKMAN *In Memoriam Vincent Persichetti*

STUCKY Concerto for Orchestra, world premiere; Constitutional Commission, underwritten by Johnson & Higgins (Philadelphia, New York)

1989–90
RANDS *Le Tambourin* Suites Nos. 1 & 2 (Philadelphia, New York: Lincoln Center)

PROKOFIEV *The Meeting of the Volga and the Don* (Philadelphia, New York)

PERGOLESI Stabat mater

CHERUBINI Requiem in C minor: Patricia Schuman, Susanne Mentzer, Westminster Symphonic Choir (Philadelphia, New York)

CASTALDO Viola Concerto, world premiere: Joseph de Pasquale

FARAGO *In Memoriam*, world premiere

1990–91
WERNICK Symphony No. 1 (Philadelphia, New York)

WUORINEN *Machault mon chou*

GIAN FRANCESCO MALIPIERO *Vivaldiana*

RANDS *Ceremonial 3*, world premiere; commissioned for The Philadelphia Orchestra by Carnegie Hall in honor of its centennial (Philadelphia, New York)

1991–92
MOZART Requiem: Arleen Auger, Susanne Mentzer, Josef Kundlák, Simon Estes, Westminster Choir (Philadelphia, New York); first subscription performance

MARTUCCI Piano Concerto No. 2: Carlo Bruno

PAGANINI Violin Concerto No. 4: Gidon Kremer

THE **1988** PERFORMANCES OF BEETHOVEN'S 9TH SYMPHONY WERE THE FIRST FOR THE MUTI/PHILADELPHIA PARTNERSHIP.

The Philadelphia Orchestra
Riccardo Muti
MUSIC DIRECTOR

Thursday Evening, April 21 at 8:00 p.m.
Friday Afternoon, April 22 at 2:00 p.m.
Saturday Evening, April 23 at 8:00 p.m.
Tuesday Eve... ...il 26 at 8:00 p.m.

Riccardo ... conducting
Cheryl Studer, ...no
Delores Ziegler, ...-soprano
Peter Seiffert, tenor
James Morris, bass
Westminster Choir
Joseph Flummerfelt, Director

MOZART/M. HAYDN   Symphony No. 37, K. 444†
BEETHOVEN   Symphony No. 9, "Choral"
†First performances by The Philadelphia Orchestra

These concerts are sponsored by The Penn Mutual Life Insurance Company.

SOLD OUT

INSTRUMENTAL &
CHAMBER MUSIC

Riccardo Muti recounts how impressed he was, from his first meeting with The Philadelphia Orchestra, by the sheer capability of the "instrument." The players are, collectively, the conductor's instrument, of course, and the symphonic repertoire is the primary means by which he and they communicate with each other and the audience.

Two particular types of instrumental repertoire require special skill: the accompaniment of soloists, and the playing of chamber music. In the first, the rapport between conductor and orchestra is put to the test of supporting a third party — the soloist — who relies on that rapport. In the second, the conductor steps aside, as small groups of instrumentalists explore the music together in the most intimate interpersonal exchange. While chamber music is not performed during the Orchestra's subscription series, a special series was established during Riccardo Muti's tenure, to provide a showcase for those Orchestra members who wished to perform that repertoire. It has become an immensely popular feature of the season, and one that adds challenge and support to the artistic life of those who participate.

ORCHESTRA ASSISTANT CONCERTMAS-
TER NANCY BEAN, ASSISTANT PRINCI-
PAL CELLO LLOYD SMITH, AND
ASSOCIATE PRINCIPAL VIOLA JAMES
FAWCETT ARE JOINED BY PIANIST
EMANUEL AX FOR ONE OF THE
PHILADELPHIA ORCHESTRA CHAMBER
MUSIC CONCERTS, 1990.

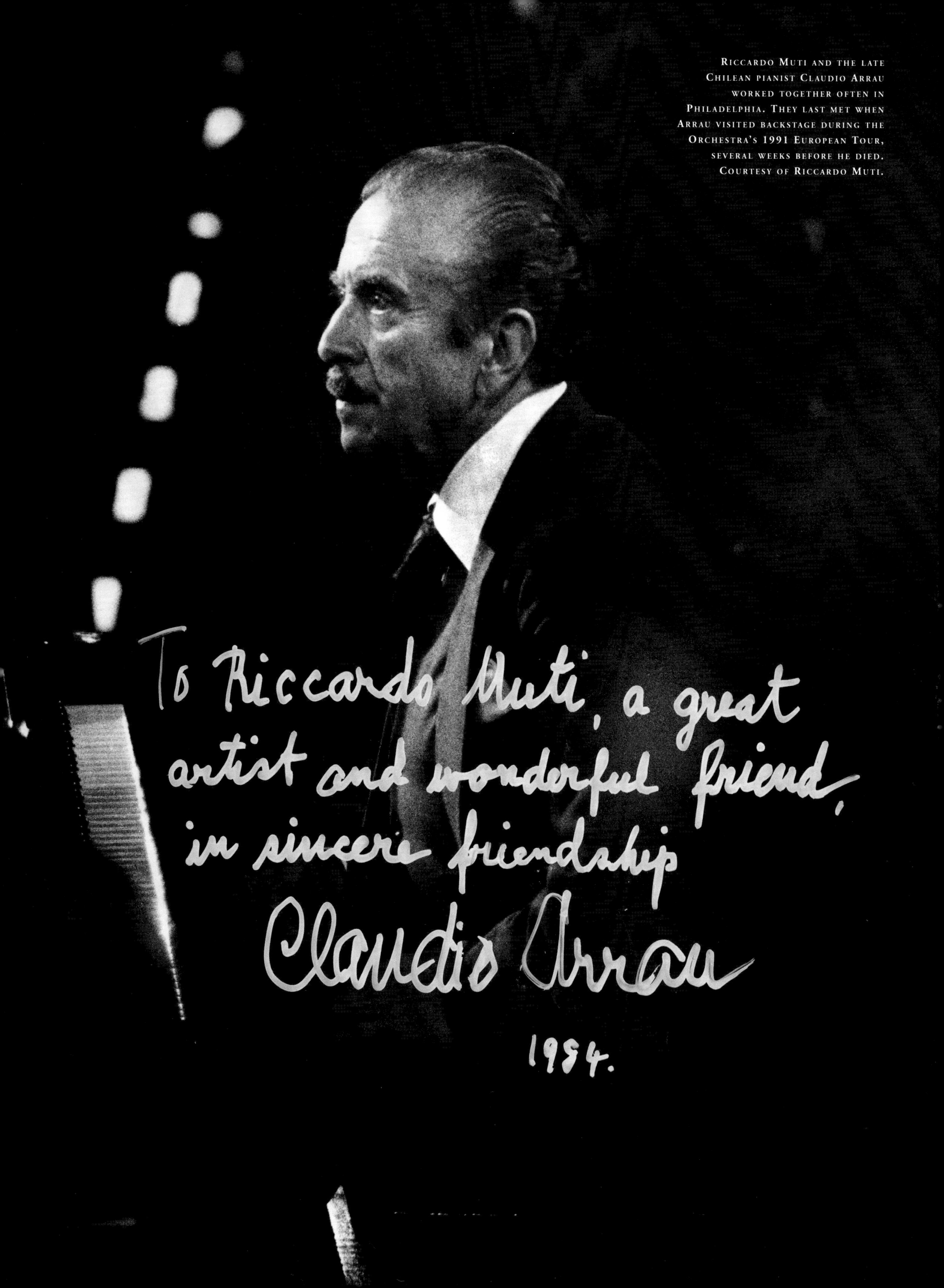

To Riccardo Muti, a great
artist and wonderful friend,
in sincere friendship
Claudio Arrau
1984.

Riccardo Muti and the late Chilean pianist Claudio Arrau worked together often in Philadelphia. They last met when Arrau visited backstage during the Orchestra's 1991 European Tour, several weeks before he died. Courtesy of Riccardo Muti.

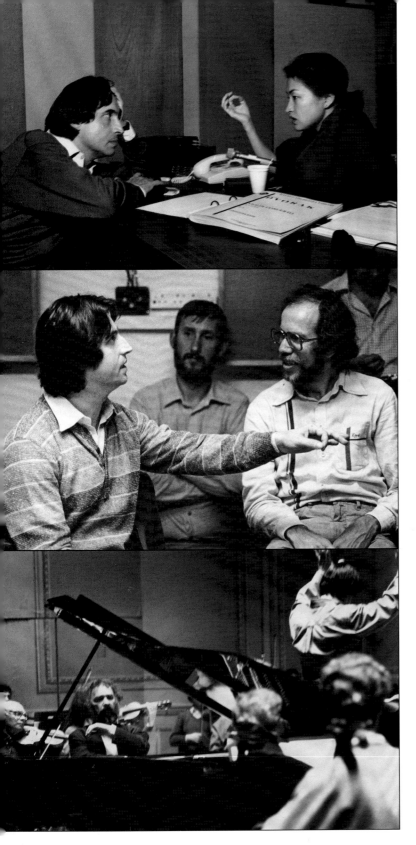

Dear Riccardo,
Every time we have worked together has been wonderful, but I will never forget how especially supportive you were during our entire experience of recording the Dvořák Violin Concerto in Philadelphia. I wish you great satisfaction wherever your career may take you, and I look forward to our future collaborations.
KYUNG-WHA CHUNG

Riccardo Muti is to me one of very few maestros around who, despite a big success, remains an honest, serious, and sincere musician. Why? I guess he still loves what music is about. ❧ *Dear Riccardo! I wish from all my heart: don't change. Remain as earnest, loyal, and charming as I have experienced you in Philadelphia and at all other places bound and unbound to it!*
GIDON KREMER

I first met Riccardo Muti in 1976 in London. It marked the beginning of our musical friendship that has lasted all this time and hopefully will continue for many more years. ❧ *We have played many concerts together, some good ones (and they were good!), some less good. In expressing my admiration for Riccardo, I would also like to say something about him that touches upon a quality that all we musicians dream to possess: leadership. I am almost convinced, for example, that if Riccardo were simply to stand in front of an orchestra, that orchestra would be unable to play badly; such is the strength of his presence and power of communication.* ❧ *In departing from The Philadelphia Orchestra, besides leaving behind both music and friends, I am sure he will miss the unique Philadelphia Orchestra jokes, but equally certain he will acquire some new ones on other shores.*
RADU LUPU

Riccardo is always completely prepared for every rehearsal and is as serious about conducting the concerto repertoire as he is about the symphonic. He devotes just as much time to it, working carefully on intonation and balancing chords. The Orchestra is always tired after he's worked with them, and although they may occasionally complain about overworking, their faces show the glow of fulfillment. In short, Riccardo is a great artistic director who is a real model for others. I, among others, am sad to see him leave.
YO-YO MA

I shall never forget the joy of playing the Bloch Concerto with The Philadelphia Orchestra and Riccardo Muti some years ago, nor the scintillating and elegant Così fan tutte *he conducted in Salzburg. I know that this wonderful musician and conductor is still going from strength to strength. You will be losing one of my favorite conductors as your music director.*
YEHUDI MENUHIN

How to thank you, Maestro, for greatly enriching our musical life through your post as Music Director of The Philadelphia Orchestra? Through a very natural, yet unique kind of music-making, allied to a discipline that doesn't stifle but rather inspires your musicians, a warmth and an honesty, you have allowed the Orchestra to build upon and diversify its already legendary achievements. Privileged on a few occasions to collaborate with your Orchestra, I have seen you, without histrionics and without fuss, build an interpretation and let it blossom. Indeed, the Orchestra has become an ever more responsive and sensitive instrument under your guidance. ❦ Heartfelt congratulations on a wonderful association that will be remembered in gratitude for years to come.
MURRAY PERAHIA

Riccardo,
Buon Viaggio! I wish to you a safe journey as you return home. We will miss you in North America and I wish you every great continued success. I am hopeful that we shall have the opportunity to work together in the future. ❦ With the greatest admiration and respect, your friend,
PINCHAS ZUKERMAN

ABOVE: REHEARSING WITH CELLIST YO-YO MA, 1988

PAGE 36: SIR YEHUDI MENUHIN WAS SOLOIST IN THE ORCHESTRA'S FIRST PERFORMANCES OF ERNST BLOCH'S VIOLIN CONCERTO IN 1982.

PAGE 37 TOP: PIANIST MAURIZIO POLLINI PLAYED BRAHMS'S CONCERTO NO. 1 IN HIS FIRST APPEARANCES WITH THE ORCHESTRA AFTER 23 YEARS, IN 1991. THE CONCERT WAS BROADCAST LIVE ON WFLN-FM DURING RADIOTHON 1991.

PAGE 37 BOTTOM: PIANO SOLOIST MURRAY PERAHIA, 1975

New York
17 Nov, 1975

To the Maestro Riccardo Muti
a great conductor with whom
I love to play. –
Zino Francescatti

The late Zino Francescatti. The
violinist was soloist for the
Mendelssohn Concerto in 1975.
Courtesy of Riccardo Muti

To Riccardo Muti with admiration and affection, Rudolf Serkin. January 1988

REHEARSING WITH THE LATE
RUDOLF SERKIN, 1987.
COURTESY OF RICCARDO MUTI

39

VOCAL MUSIC

REHEARSING THE WESTMINSTER SYMPHONIC CHOIR

Like many great conductors of previous generations, Riccardo Muti received some of his earliest training and experience as a vocal coach. The insight he gained into the nature of the "singing line" of music became essential to his work with instrumentalists as well as vocalists.

In Philadelphia, Muti conducted at least one major vocal work each season from the time of his appointment as Principal Guest Conductor. The first two were works by Prokofiev: *Ivan the Terrible* and *Alexander Nevsky*, and both were also performed in New York. Muti came full circle when he chose *Alexander Nevsky* for the Orchestra's program for the Gala Opening Night of Carnegie Hall's 1988–89 season. In between came an array of interesting and diverse works. Among those new to the Orchestra season, surprisingly, was Mozart's Requiem, which he "introduced" to subscription audiences in 1991. But for many listeners the most memorable vocal contribution of Muti was his revival of the practice of performing complete operas in concert form. Its impact was summarized by *Philadelphia Inquirer* critic Daniel Webster in a 1991 column:

"Muti can point to a list of operatic performances that have had musical and historical significance. His dedication to authentic texts has led him to perform American premieres of the critical editions of Verdi's *Nabucco* and *Rigoletto*, and Puccini's *Tosca*. He often used those and his other operas — Verdi's *Macbeth*, Gluck's *Orfeo ed Euridice*, and Wagner's *Der fliegende Holländer* — to introduce singers, many of them Americans not widely known here but already recognized as specialists in their parts.

"By casting the Orchestra in opera, and by using that casting to open opera to the critical scrutiny of audiences aware of Muti's search for the pristine text and musical detail, Muti has made these almost annual forays into opera part of the intellectual life of the city.

"The Orchestra has not always been part of that life. Muti's achievement has been musical, theatrical, and philosophical, a considerable achievement in any setting."

SOLOISTS ARLEEN AUGER AND SUSANNE MENTZER ARE
SHOWN DURING THE ORCHESTRA'S FIRST SUBSCRIPTION
PERFORMANCES OF MOZART'S REQUIEM, IN 1991. THIS
PERFORMANCE, ALSO FEATURING JOSEF KUNDLÁK, SIMON
ESTES, AND THE WESTMINSTER SYMPHONIC CHOIR, WAS
BROADCAST LIVE ON KYW-TV3 AND WHYY RADIO.

Dear Riccardo,

*Twenty years ago when you began your association with The Philadel-
phia Orchestra, I began my own musical association with you performing Mozart. It was during the Maggio Musicale in Firenze that we
met. Although I had already had the good fortune to work with many
great conductors, singing Mozart with most of them, I will always treasure the memory of the pure joy and exhilaration in our first music-
making together.* ❧ *As I sang that day, you leaned back, and with a
warm, smiling face you "accompanied" my voice with your orchestra. In
an instant we were as dear companions, gently and caringly guiding
each other through the secret garden filled with beauty and light.* ❧ *We
have often worked together since, and I have always felt privileged to be*

*able to continue experiencing this unique musical fulfillment with you,
Riccardo. I cherish all these exquisite moments as the rarest of gifts
which flow from within you. These are the most precious rewards an
artist could ever hope to receive for the dedication we owe to our profession.* ❧ *With great affection,*
ARLEEN AUGER

To Maestro Muti,

*With appreciation for bringing me "home" to The Philadelphia Orchestra
and for your continuing encouragement and inspiration.* ❧ *Each musical
experience I have had with you has been like an incredible journey.*
SUSANNE MENTZER LANDMESSER

Dear Maestro,

May I add my voice to those of many Philadelphians who sing your praises, who regret your leaving, and who wish you well. ❧ *You have opened minds and ears in your uncompromising approach to music. Your relentless search for the truthful spirit of the music is exemplary, and we are your debtors.*

ELAINE BROWN, *Conductor Laureate, Singing City*

Dear Maestro Muti!

On behalf of all my singers in the Choral Arts Society, I thank you, deeply, for the many opportunities to share your musical vision: Opening Night at Carnegie Hall with Alexander Nevsky, *Jessye Norman and the (Brahms)* Alto Rhapsody, *your deeply felt spiritual convictions and reflections on the Verdi Requiem, and our many other wonderful collaborations. You have touched so many hearts!* ❧ *Your personal generosity of spirit and time with me have made for unforgettable moments!*

SEÁN DEIBLER, *Artistic Director, Choral Arts Society of Philadelphia*

Maestro Muti and I were born in the same year, I just six months earlier. Over the years he teased me about being older, and I would tell him he would never be able to catch up with me. But in a certain way our careers grew up together, just as our lives were shaped in different, yet parallel ways. It is rare when a great musician with first rate talent and first rate ability continues to fight for further growth and development after he has been recognized as one of the greatest in the history of the conducting profession. This ever-evolving quality, always deepening in humanity, is what makes Riccardo so special to me. ❧ *So many wonderful collaborations are close to my heart; thrilling evenings in Milano, Vienna, and Munich, and many, many rewarding times in the recording studio.* ❧ *Of course I regret seeing Maestro Muti leave Philadelphia, and among other reasons, we won't be able to realize our plans for now to do* Otello *with the Orchestra.* ❧ *I had the pleasure years ago to work with Eugene Ormandy, and now that Riccardo Muti leaves after having so fully developed your unique tradition, I share with your joy in the celebration of a great era, and I share your sorrow that life always must move on.*

PLACIDO DOMINGO

Dear Riccardo,

Westminster Choir College and its students have been deeply affected by our many very special performances with The Philadelphia Orchestra. Your profound musicality, your passionate pursuit of the meaning behind the sound and, of course, your great orchestra have made every collaboration a joyful occasion. ❧ *Thank you for all the wonderful music-making. Best wishes in the exciting years that lie ahead of you. I hope our personal and musical paths may cross often.*

JOSEPH FLUMMERFELT, *Artistic Director and Principal Conductor, Westminster Choir College*

I admit it. For me, to speak of Riccardo Muti is to repeat all the wonderful things that have been written and said about him. I therefore can't add anything, other than that we have before us one of today's most authoritative conductors. His baton, in its clarity of gesture, quality of execution, and conducting capability, accompanies a musicological experience put to the service of the the most respectful observation of the score. That is how he seemed to me when I first met him in the studios of the Italian radio in Rome for a radio broadcast of I Puritani. It was followed by Ernani, Don Pasquale, and La forza del destino. Each time, Riccardo Muti's personality gave proof of music-making that was cultured, modern, exemplary, without compromise, even when he led the entire La Scala cast of Ernani from the piano, at a benefit concert in Ravenna. ❧ After all this, I would like to say, dear Maestro, that it has always been a great joy for me to make music with you. I wish for you and the marvelous Philadelphia Orchestra the greatest success always. ❧ With my highest esteem,
MIRELLA FRENI

Lo confesso. Parlare di Riccardo Muti, per me, è come ripetere le tante belle cose che si sono dette e scritte di lui. Non posso dunque aggiungere nulla, se non che siamo di fronte a un maestro direttore dei più autorevoli delle generazioni di musicisti contemporanei. Una bachetta che, al valore esecutivo, al gesto chiaro, alla capacità di concertatore, accompagna una pratica filologica messa al servizio della più rispettosa osservanza dei testi che è chiamato ad interpretare. ❧ Tale mi è parso—e non è certamente una mia scoperta— quando lo incontrai, per la prima volta, negli studi della Radio nazionale italiana, a Roma. L'occasione fu una esecuzione radiofonica de I Puritani *di Vincenzo Bellini. Seguirono, poi* Ernani, Don Pasquale, e La forza del destino *di Verdi. Sempre, la personalità di Riccardo Muti ha dato prova di un modo di "fare musica" colto, moderno, esemplare, sensa compromessi, anche quando, come pianista, guidò l'intera compagnia dell'* Ernani *scaligero, in un concerto di beneficenza a Ravenna. ❧ Dopo questa chiaccherata, mi permetta di dirLe, caro maestro, che per me è stata sempre una grande gioia fare musica insieme. Augurando a Lei e alla meravigliosa orchestra di Filadelfia sempre grandi ed infiniti successi. ❧ Con tutta la mia stima,*
MIRELLA FRENI

DEMONSTRATING A POINT DURING ONE OF HIS PUBLIC DISCUSSIONS ABOUT OPERA, 1986

Riccardo Muti has brought to The Philadelphia Orchestra, and indeed to the musical life of the United States, a unique perspective on opera. Although a number of conductors working with major American orchestras have also conducted opera extensively, none has insisted with such conviction that a symphonic orchestra needs the experience of playing opera in order fully to develop its skills. ❧ I have had the privilege of working with Maestro Muti on a number of these projects in my capacity as general editor of the new editions of the works of Verdi and Rossini, and I can say without exaggeration that there are no conductors working today who have approached their works with greater love or conviction. There has been widespread confusion about the meaning of Maestro Muti's belief that the music should be performed according to the score, not following the guide of a dubious "tradition." In no way, however, does this diminish the role of the interpreter. Every note a musician plays requires an act of interpretation. Under Muti's baton, however, the interpretation grows from the score, rather than being imposed on it, and singers who have worked with him in projects such as Rigoletto *or* Nabucco *have communicated to me their joy at being part of these events. ❧ Nor can I ever forget those wonderful "performances" (what else can I call them?) with Muti illustrating the operas at the piano, stalking around the stage, singing all the high notes he refused to allow his singers to interpolate, mugging, clowning, and yet making a very serious point about the respect we owed to the music of Verdi. Unforgettable! ❧ I hope that the combination Riccardo Muti and The Philadelphia Orchestra will continue, even if only from time to time, to keep the magic alive.*
PHILIP GOSSETT, *Dean, Division of the Humanities, The University of Chicago*

I first met Riccardo Muti in the late 70s in Florence after he had directed a splendid Trovatore. *The first meeting was quite unusual in that he attacked me verbally. His complaints were due to a series of negative coincidences and our barely formed editorial policy on the literary study of Itslian opera. But it was eventually from this ground that grew, like our old adage, "the calm after the storm," an intellectual and moral rapport of great importance to me.* ❧ *Riccardo Muti followed with passion and infinitely meticulous interpretive seriousness many of the critical editions of Verdi and Rossini that Ricordi published with The University of Chicago Press and the Fondazione Rossini.* ❧ *To experience the results of this musicological research in his performances, which can shape new and vast dramatic horizons, is a continuous stimulus to the editor and a great relief from the stresses of daily life. For this we are infinitely grateful to him.*

MIMMA GUASTONI, *General Editorial Director, G. Ricordi & Co.*

Conobbi Riccardo Muti alla fine degli anni '70 a Firenze dopo uno splendido Trovatore *da lui diretto. Il primo incontro fu quanto mai bizzarro, mi aggredì, verbalmente è vero. Una serie di concidenze negative e una politica editoriale ancora ai suoi inizi nel settore della rilettura filologica del melodramma italiano avevano suscitato le sue rimostranze. Ma fu propio quest'ultimo il terreno su cui è nato poi, secondo il vecchio adagio "il sereno dopo la tempesta", un rapporto intelletuale e morale di grande importanza per me.* ❧ *Riccardo Muti ha seguito con infinita passione e meticolosa serietà interpretativa molte delle edizioni critiche verdiane e rossiniane che Ricordi edita rispettivamente con la University of Chicago Press e la Fondazione Rossini.* ❧ *Verificare il lavoro musicologico nella viva realtà delle sue interpretazioni, capaci di ricostruire atmosfere e orizzonti drammaturgici nuovi e vasti, è di continuo stimolo all'editore ed un grande sollievo alle fatiche del quotidiano. Gliene siamo infinitamente grati.*

MIMMA GUASTONI, *Direttore Generale Editoriale, G. Ricordi & Co.*

Dear Maestro Muti,

I am proud to have been a part of some of the work you have done during your long affiliation with The Philadelphia Orchestra. Your meticulous attention to detail has affected and will continue to affect the way in which I prepare and present myself throughout my artistic career. Your expectation of one hundred percent from your colleagues is only surpassed by the one hundred and ten percent which you yourself contribute to every performance. ❧ *I congratulate you on your twenty years with The Philadelphia Orchestra and wish you continued success in all your future endeavors.*

FRANK LOPARDO

Since our first collaboration at the Maggio Musicale (Florence, 1970), I have had the great privilege of exploring a very varied repertoire with Riccardo Muti: The music of Handel, Meyerbeer, Mahler, Berlioz, Rossini, and Verdi, all so different, yet all illuminated to the fullest under the Maestro's considered and expert direction. I offer my congratulations on the outstanding music-making with the Philadelphians and extend my best wishes for the future, and eternal admiration and love.

JESSYE NORMAN

Caro Riccardo,

Venti anni di collaborazione sono un bel pezzo di vita. Vita spesa al servizio della musica ai più alti livelli. BRAVO! Mancherai certamente a tutti. ❧ *Un caro saluto,*

LUCIANO PAVAROTTI

Twenty years of collaboration make an impressive slice of life. A life spent in the service of music at the highest levels. BRAVO! You will certainly be missed by all. ❧ *With fond greetings,*
LUCIANO PAVAROTTI

There are thousands in Philadelphia and elsewhere in this country who are grateful for the way you have enriched their lives through your music-making. I'm one of those thousands, because I've been part of your audience. But more than that, I thank you for the privilege and joy of making music with you. Every performance under your guidance has been a milestone for me.

SAMUEL RAMEY

Dear Riccardo,

I want to express my congratulations for the wonderful work that, throughout the years, you have accomplished with The Philadelphia Orchestra. It was a great pleasure for me to experience the wonderful artistic moments with you that will remain unforgettable. ❧ *With all my sincere affection,*

RENATA SCOTTO

Dearest Maestro,

In sending you my warmest congratulations on this occasion, I wish to thank you. I wish to thank you for your unrelenting determination. Thank you for your musical integrity. Thank you for your uncompromising dedication. Thank you for your support and belief in me. Thank you for your wit and good humor! Thank you for not only having inspired me during our artistic collaborations with The Philadelphia Orchestra and Teatro alla Scala, but for having influenced my basic understanding of music, which has reflected on my musical activities elsewhere and will continue to guide me throughout my life. I consider myself extremely fortunate to have had so many musical encounters with you. I can only hope that as many of my colleagues as possible will be able to profit, as I have, from working with you — if only briefly. Needless to say, I also look forward to our future projected plans with the greatest of expectations! ❧ In deepest appreciation and dedication, I remain sincerely yours,

CHERYL L. STUDER

Working with Maestro Muti has been one of the most personal and rewarding experiences of my career. Our performances together in Philadelphia, Salzburg, and at La Scala have all aspired to the highest possible quality, and it has been Maestro Muti who consistently demanded my best. ❧ I look forward to many more years to come.

CAROL VANESS

Lucky Philadelphia, lucky U.S.A. to have Maestro Muti for this period. Lucky all of us to work with him.

FREDERICA VON STADE

CONCERT OPERAS AND MAJOR CHORAL WORKS CONDUCTED BY RICCARDO MUTI

1977-78

PROKOFIEV *Ivan the Terrible*: Claudine Carlson, Boris Carmeli, Mendelssohn Club (Philadelphia, New York)

1978-79

PROKOFIEV *Alexander Nevsky*: Florence Quivar, Mendelssohn Club (Philadelphia, New York)

1979-80

VERDI Requiem: Katia Ricciarelli, Agnes Baltsa, Veriano Luchetti, Simon Estes, Mendelssohn Club (Philadelphia, New York). A performance was also taped in Philadelphia's Cathedral Basilica of Saints Peter and Paul for national television broadcast.

1980-81

MOZART Mass in C minor: Gwendolyn Bradley, Agnes Baltsa, Neil Rosenshein, Paul Plishka, Singing City Choir (Philadelphia, New York)

SCRIABIN Symphony No. 1: Beverly Wolff, Jon Fredric West, Mendelssohn Club (Philadelphia, New York)

1981–82

STRAVINSKY *Symphony of Psalms*: Mendelssohn Club (Philadelphia, New York)

CHERUBINI Requiem in C Minor: Mendelssohn Club. First performance by The Philadelphia Orchestra (Philadelphia, New York)

1982–83

BERLIOZ *Roméo et Juliette* (complete): Beverly Wolff, Philip Creech, Simon Estes, Singing City Choir

1983–84

VERDI *Macbeth*, U.S. premiere of critical edition: Renato Bruson, Elizabeth Connell, Simon Estes, Westminster Symphonic Choir (Philadelphia, New York). Orchestra's first complete opera performances in 50 years. Initiates Opera Week, an educational outreach program including public discussion between Muti and opera scholars, and special public rehearsals for the opera.

ORFF *Carmina Burana*: Arleen Auger, Ruediger Wohlers, Claudio Desderi, Westminster Symphonic Choir, Philadelphia Boys Choir

1984–85

GLUCK *Orfeo ed Euridice* (original 1762 version): Agnes Baltsa, Margaret Marshall, Arleen Auger, Westminster Choir (Philadelphia, New York). Opera Week includes screenings of classic 1959 Marcel Camus film *Black Orpheus*.

SCRIABIN Symphony No. 1: Stefania Toczyska, Jon Fredric West, Westminster Symphonic Choir

VERDI Requiem, Memorial Concert for Eugene Ormandy: Carol Vaness, Diane Curry, Luis Lima, Paul Plishka, members of the Choral Arts Society, Singing City, and Temple University choruses

1985–86

VERDI *Rigoletto*, U.S. premiere of new critical edition: Renato Bruson, Cecilia Gasdia, Michael Myers, Westminster Choir (Philadelphia, New York). Opera Week includes round table discussion with international panel of critics and musicologists.

BACH Mass in B minor, in honor of composer's 300th-anniversary year: Margaret Marshall, Anne Sofie von Otter, Keith Lewis, Wolfgang Schoene, Singing City Choir

1986–87

BERLIOZ *Roméo et Juliette*: Jessye Norman, John Aler, Simon Estes, Westminster Choir

WAGNER *Der fliegende Holländer*: Aage Haugland, Hartmut Welker, Sabine Hass, Gary Lakes, Michael Myers, Clarity James, Westminster Symphonic Choir. Opera Week includes discussion with musicologists Roman Vlad and Bernard Jacobson.

1987–88

MOZART *Ave verum corpus*: Westminster Choir (Philadelphia, New York)

BRUCKNER *Te Deum*: Maria Fortuna, Gweneth Bean, Frank Lopardo, Mark Doss, Westminster Choir (Philadelphia, New York)

VERDI *Quattro pezzi sacri*: Maria Fortuna, Westminster Choir (Philadelphia, New York)

BEETHOVEN Symphony No. 9, *Choral*: Cheryl Studer, Delores Ziegler, Peter Seiffert, James Morris, Westminster Symphonic Choir

1988–89

PROKOFIEV *Alexander Nevsky*: Alexandrina Milcheva, Choral Arts Society (Philadelphia, New York)

VERDI *Nabucco*, U.S. premiere of critical edition: Linda Roark-Strummer, Michael Myers, Paata Burchuladze, Westminster Choir (Philadelphia, New York)

1989–90

PERGOLESI Stabat mater: Patricia Schuman, Susanne Mentzer (Philadelphia, New York)

CHERUBINI Requiem in C minor: Westminster Symphonic Choir (Philadelphia, New York)

1990–91

PUCCINI *Tosca*: Carol Vaness, Giuseppe Giacomini, Giorgio Zancanaro, Danilo Serraiocco, Westminster Choir, Philadelphia Boys Choir

1991–92

MOZART Requiem: Arleen Auger, Susanne Mentzer, Josef Kundlák, Simon Estes, Westminster Symphonic Choir (Philadelphia, New York). Broadcast live on KYW-TV3

LEONCAVALLO *Pagliacci*: Luciano Pavarotti, Daniela Dessì, Juan Pons, Paolo Coni, Ernesto Gavazzi, Westminster Symphonic Choir, Philadelphia Boys Choir (Philadelphia, New York)

ROSSINI Stabat mater: Carol Vaness, Delores Ziegler, Chris Merritt, Roberto Scandiuzzi, Philadelphia Singers Chorale

CONTEMPORARY MUSIC

MAESTRO MUTI WORKS WITH CHRISTOPHER ROUSE, COMPOSER OF *PHAETHON*, THE FIRST OF THE CONSTITUTIONAL COMMISSIONS. MAESTRO MUTI AND THE ORCHESTRA GAVE ITS WORLD PREMIERE IN 1987.

In the spring of 1983, Riccardo Muti and Pulitzer Prize-winning composer Richard Wernick met for the first time. They discovered quickly that they held two basic views in common: firstly, that The Philadelphia Orchestra, as a world-class institution, had a responsibility to perform the music of its own time on a regular basis and should emphasize American music while maintaining its international outlook. Secondly, all contemporary music should be performed in subscription concerts in the context of the standard repertoire, and not, as some other American orchestras do, as separate programs or "festivals."

Maestro Muti named Wernick, a professor at the University of Pennsylvania, as the Orchestra's Consultant for Contemporary Music. In 1989, Bernard Rands was appointed Composer-in-Residence under the auspices of the national Meet the Composer program, continuing the advisory activities that Mr. Wernick had undertaken. The Orchestra has made a commitment to continue working with a composer-in-residence even after its arrangement with Meet the Composer ends in 1993.

Since the opening of the 1983–84 season, The Philadelphia Orchestra has performed nearly 100 pieces of contemporary music, most of them by American composers; has commissioned a dozen, and given the world premieres of more than fifteen, all as part of the regular subscription series. Celebrating the 200th anniversary of the United States Constitution, it commissioned six new works with a generous grant from Johnson & Higgins, known as the Constitutional Commissions. It has given repeat performances of significant American compositions under the auspices of the AT&T American Encore series, and it is in the midst of a three-year AT&T Retrospective, honoring those works which were given their world or American premieres by The Philadelphia Orchestra on the stage of the Academy of Music. Under Riccardo Muti, the Orchestra has received national recognition, including two ASCAP awards, for the contribution it has made, and continues to make, as a leader in producing the music of its own time.

In the years of our friendship, I have never once been able to think about creativity either in general philosophical notions or in my personal struggle to understand and shape specific musical ideas, without thinking of you. Why? Because you offer your innate musicality, keen intellect, profound spirit, and supremely refined skills to the service and glory of music in its search for and expression of truth. ❧ In this, you are a composer's closest and most precious friend — not only in the bright light of the concert stage, but in the intimate moment of personal solitude, which is the moment of creation. This you know, understand, and respect with your whole being and thus, were they alive today, Monteverdi, Pergolesi, Cherubini, Mozart, Schubert, Beethoven, Brahms, Verdi, Scriabin, Puccini, Mahler, Debussy, Stravinsky, Bartók, Prokofiev… would recognize in you the courage and integrity which mark their noblest musical thoughts. ❧ Your compatriot poet, Salvatore Quasimodo, though he may have had other things in mind, poignantly alludes to this in his lines:

> *Ognuno sta solo sul cuor della terra*
> *trafitto da un raggio di sole:*
> *ed é súbito sera.*

A composer and a conductor must stand alone on the heart of the earth, for only then can they be pierced through by a ray of sunlight, experiencing the excitement of ideas, glimpsing inspiration. Thus, evening brings a mature calm and the possibility for a dignified and profound utterance. ❧ These are great gifts you have bestowed on us in Philadelphia. I, as a composer, am deeply grateful that you have embraced music of our own time with the same integrity, conviction, meticulous care, and intelligence that you bring to the music of our predecessors. ❧ For me personally, your example and your friendship are indeed "un raggio di sole."

BERNARD RANDS, *the Orchestra's Composer-in-Residence*

Caro Riccardo,

What an impossible task! To compress into a small space the experiences and feelings of eight years? Those eight years are a lifetime, and words suddenly become such a weak vehicle as the memories return. You and I have had such a time looking at music together and talking about music and art and life; planning the many projects on which we collaborated; and sharing our thoughts about those things that make living in this not-so-best of all possible worlds bearable and wonderful. Those times together, and the thrilling performances you gave of my music, I will always cherish and never forget. Nor will I ever forget that your friendship and wisdom helped me through the darkest period of my life, a time when love and music became the only weapons of survival. ❧ It has been a wonderful source of joy to me, as well as to Beatrice, Lew, and Adam, that you and Cristina have touched our lives so closely. We will continue to look forward to much laughter and warm companionship. And above all, I look forward to the music, and the spirit of music, that you will continue to bring to us. Music is an incredibly powerful life force; it is the force from which our friendship sprang, and through which it is my deepest wish that it may continue.

RICHARD WERNICK, *Composer and the Orchestra's Consultant for Contemporary Music 1983–89 and Special Consultant to the Music Director*

Like everyone else, I have received from Riccardo Muti an endless number of wonderful musical presents: from Gluck to Mozart to Verdi to Beethoven to Stravinsky, from Wagner to Berlioz to Cherubini to Gluck to Brahms, from Mozart to Schumann to Verdi to Tchaikovsky to Schubert, from Vivaldi to Wagner to Rossini to Ravel to Schubert to Cherubini, from Verdi to Prokofiev to Beethoven to Moussorgsky to Mozart...It can be a lonely listener or an audience, a performer or an orchestra: everybody always has something to receive and to learn from Riccardo Muti.

LUCIANO BERIO

Best wishes to Maestro Muti from WITOLD LUTOSLAWSKI!

Devo al Maestro Riccardo Muti una delle emozioni più intense che ho provato ascoltando una mia musica. E' stata un'esecuzione del mio Coro di morti *al Teatro alla Scala di Milano, esecuzione concentrata nella spiritualità del testo letterario. La musica arrivava allo spirito degli ascoltatori, illuminando la profondità della poesia leopardiana.* ❧ *Il Maestro Muti arriva al cuore della musica stessa, traguardo che è dato a pochissimi eletti di raggiungere. Riccardo Muti è fra questi eletti rarissimi ed io personalmente devo a lui la gratitudine non soltanto per l'episodio della Scala, ma per tutte le sue esecuzioni che ho avuto modo di ascoltare e che mi hanno ogni volta esaltato, perchè raggiungevamo la verità della musica stessa.*

GOFFREDO PETRASSI

Dear Maestro Muti,

I am writing to express my profound sense of gratitude for giving me the opportunity to compose my Symphony for The Philadelphia Orchestra, and for making it possible for me to hear the fruit of my labor so beautifully brought to life by your magnificent ensemble. ❧ *May I share the satisfaction and sense of gratification of winning the 1991 Pulitzer Prize for music for Symphony with you and with the entire Philadelphia Orchestra family. Surely you must know that your commissioning program serves as a stellar example to other orchestras throughout the country!* ❧ *Above all, thank you for your faith in my work. It will always be with me.*

SHULAMIT RAN

I owe to Maestro Muti one of the most intense emotional experiences in hearing my own music. It was a performance of my Coro di morti *at La Scala, a performance intensely concentrated on the spirituality of the text. The music reached the souls of the listeners, illuminating the depth of Leopardi poetry.* ❧ *Maestro Muti strikes at the heart of music itself, an objective that few can achieve. He is among this rare elite, and I personally owe him gratitude not only for the La Scala experience, but for all the performances that have uplifted me every time, because we were brought to the essence of the music itself.*

GOFFREDO PETRASSI

Oggi vi sono esecutori perfetti ma assai pochi interpreti. Assumere e trasformare la tradizione non è di tutti: rendere vivo, in una delle sue infinite potenzialità, ciò che tuttavia in sé vita non ha, trasmetterne agli altri lo stupore. ❧ *Cultura è atto sempre personale e di coraggio insieme, civilissimo piacere erede dell'antico convito.* ❧ *Dire in breve di Muti è per me dire di queste cose, con animo amico.*

SALVATORE SCIARRINO

Dear Riccardo,

Our relationship starting with my Symphonie Concertante, which led to friendship, is one that I will always treasure as long as I live. ❧ *Since I was brought up on The Philadelphia Orchestra, I have a special soft spot for it and had hoped that someday I would write a work for it. You gave me that opportunity. I will always be grateful. Above and beyond the personal things, you made it sound magnificent, and I know that the Orchestra will miss you very much. I wish you the best in the rest of your life.*

RALPH SHAPEY, *Composer and Music Director, Contemporary Chamber Players of The University of Chicago*

Dear Maestro Muti,

While I was writing my Concerto for Orchestra, from fall 1986 to spring 1987, I had constantly in mind the fact that not only would it be played by the great Philadelphia Orchestra, but that you would conduct. I knew you were famous for studying every new score minutely, that nowhere in the third clarinet or the fourth horn could I hide a moment of slack inspi-

Today there are many fine performers but few true interpreters. Not everyone can take on and transform tradition. To bring to life, in one of its infinite possibilities, that which of itself has no life, transports others with astonishment. ❧ *Culture is always a personal statement and an act of courage, a civilized pleasure inherited from the ancient "convito."* ❧ *In short, to speak of Muti is to speak of these things, as a kindred spirit.*

SALVATORE SCIARRINO

The poster reads:

The Philadelphia Orchestra
Riccardo Muti
MUSIC DIRECTOR

AT&T American Encore

Bernard Rands
"Madrigali"

Leonard Bernstein
"Serenade for Violin,
Strings and Percussion"

Elliott Carter
"Elegy"

Jacob Druckman
"Aureole"

Irving Fine
"Symphony"

Karel Husa
"Music for Prague, 1968"

ANNOUNCING PHILADELPHIA'S PARTICIPATION IN AT&T'S
AMERICAN ENCORE PROGRAM ARE (L.) JAMES GINTY, VICE
PRESIDENT OF PHILADELPHIA, NEW JERSEY, AND DELAWARE
AT&T, AND THE LATE STEPHEN SELL, EXECUTIVE DIRECTOR
OF THE PHILADELPHIA ORCHESTRA FROM 1982–89. INITIATED
IN 1986, THE PROGRAM PROVIDED FOR WIDER EXPOSURE OF
20TH-CENTURY WORKS ALREADY PERFORMED.

ration or a patch of weak invention. I don't think I have ever worked harder on any piece to be worthy of the kind of interpretive powers I had heard you bring to older repertoire. Thus your presence looming over me as I worked had a real and lasting effect on me as a composer. ❧ The premiere of the Concerto for Orchestra in October 1988 will remain one of the great experiences of my musical life. The Orchestra played wonderfully, but what I will remember most is how thoroughly and deeply you understood the score (indeed, how gracious you were to work with). ❧ All over the United States, musicians have felt secure in the knowledge that one of our greatest musical institutions, The Philadelphia Orchestra, was in the best possible hands — and not only for the European repertoire of the nineteenth century, but for the music of our time and of our people as well.... You have done a great and lasting service not just to Philadelphia but to American music. When I think of you now, it is not with trepidation but with gratitude — and still, perhaps, a little awe.

STEVEN STUCKY, *Composer-in-Residence,*
Los Angeles Philharmonic Orchestra

Maestro Riccardo Muti will be remembered by Philadelphia for many things, mostly for taking our cherished Orchestra to a new level of worldwide fame. But he also pushed the Orchestra and its admirers into new and challenging music, perhaps best represented by the Constitutional Commissions, which our firm underwrote in 1985. ❧ When the new home of the Orchestra opens its doors in the next few years, many of us who were there at the beginning of the dream will remember that the Maestro's keen interest in creating the desperately needed facility was a persuasive factor in the decision to move ahead. ❧ So, we will miss his leadership of both our hearts and our minds in the linkage of our present and future. He will be gone, but never forgotten.

RODNEY D. DAY III, *Regional Director, Northeast Region,*
Johnson & Higgins

It was an honor to initiate AT&T's American Encore Series and Retrospective Celebration with The Philadelphia Orchestra under your leadership. With courage, you brought to these programs and to the repertoire of the Orchestra imagination, innovation, and a creativity that will remain as a heritage of your term as Music Director. ❧ Carol and I will miss you. We wish you the very best.

JAMES B. GINTY, *Vice President, Pennsylvania, New Jersey, and*
Delaware AT&T

WORLD PREMIERES DURING RICCARDO MUTI'S TENURE AS MUSIC DIRECTOR

(*conducted by Maestro Muti)

1980–81

DAVID DEL TREDICI *All in the Golden Afternoon*: Benita Valente; commissioned by Eugene Ormandy and The Philadelphia Orchestra with the assistance of a grant from the Atlantic Richfield Foundation

EZRA LADERMAN Violin Concerto: Elmar Oliveira

ANDRÉ PREVIN *Reflections* for English Horn, Cello, and Orchestra: Louis Rosenblatt, William Stokking; commissioned by the Saratoga Performing Arts Center

1982–83

*EZRA LADERMAN Concerto for Flute, Bassoon, and Orchestra: Murray Panitz, Bernard Garfield; commissioned by The Philadelphia Orchestra in connection with the 300th anniversary of the City of Philadelphia (Philadelphia, Washington, D.C.)

1983–84

SERGEI RACHMANINOFF/BUKETOFF Act I of *Monna Vanna*; Sherrill Milnes, Henry Grossman, Nicholas Karousatos, John Alexander, Tatiana Troyanos, Saratoga-Potsdam Chorus (Saratoga Performing Arts Center)

1984–85

*RAYMOND PREMRU Music for Three Trombones, Tuba, and Orchestra: Glenn Dodson, L. David Read, Charles Vernon, Paul Krzywicki; commissioned by the West Philadelphia Committee for The Philadelphia Orchestra (Philadelphia, New York)

1985–86

STANISLAW SKROWACZEWSKI Violin Concerto: Norman Carol; commissioned by the Old York Road Committee for The Philadelphia Orchestra

*RICHARD WERNICK Violin Concerto: Gregory Fulkerson (The work won the 1986 Friedheim Award.)

1986–87

*CHRISTOPHER ROUSE *Phaethon*; Constitutional Commission, underwritten by Johnson & Higgins (Philadelphia, New York)

*RALPH SHAPEY Symphonie Concertante; Constitutional Commission, underwritten by Johnson & Higgins (Philadelphia, New York)

CHINARY UNG *Inner Voices*; commissioned by the Pennsylvania Council on the Arts (The work won the 1989 Grawemeyer Award.)

STANLEY WALDEN *Invisible Cities*; Constitutional Commission, underwritten by Johnson & Higgins (Philadelphia, New York)

1987–88

NICHOLAS THORNE *Revelations*; Constitutional Commission, underwritten by Johnson & Higgins

1988–89

*STEVEN STUCKY Concerto for Orchestra; Constitutional Commission, underwritten by Johnson & Higgins (Philadelphia, New York)

1989–90

WILLIAM BOLCOM Fifth Symphony; commissioned by The Philadelphia Orchestra

*JOSEPH CASTALDO Viola Concerto: Joseph de Pasquale

MARIO DAVIDOVSKY Concertante for String Quartet and Orchestra: Guarneri Quartet; commissioned by The Philadelphia Orchestra (Philadelphia, New York)

*MARCEL FARAGO *In Memoriam*

1990–91

DARON HAGEN Symphony No. 1

SHULAMIT RAN Symphony; commissioned by The Philadelphia Orchestra, funded by the Rivera-Price Music Foundation and the Rittenhouse Square Committee for The Philadelphia Orchestra (The work won the 1991 Pulitzer Prize.)

*BERNARD RANDS *Ceremonial 3*; commissioned for The Philadelphia Orchestra by Carnegie Hall in honor of its Centennial (Philadelphia, New York)

AUGUSTA READ THOMAS *Glass Moon*

1991–92

STEPHEN ALBERT *Wind Canticle*: David Shifrin; commission made possible by a grant from the Meet the Composer/Reader's Digest Commissioning Program, in partnership with the National Endowment for the Arts and the Lila Wallace-Reader's Digest Fund

RETROSPECTIVE ENCOUNTERS

Since the 1990 season, the AT&T Retrospective series has featured works that were originally given their world or U.S. premieres by The Philadelphia Orchestra. Retrospective Encounters recall the premieres of these works by interviewing eyewitnesses of the premieres and other guest speakers immediately after the performances.

1990–91

VERESE Arcana

BARBER Violin Concerto

GINASTERA Harp Concerto

RACHMANINOFF Symphonic Dances

RACHMANINOFF Symphony No. 3

SIBELIUS Symphony No. 7

BARTÓK Piano Concerto No. 3

SCRIABIN *Le Divin poème*

GLUCK Overture to *Iphigenie en Aulide*

1991–92

BARBER *Medea's Dance of Vengeance*

STRAVINSKY Symphonies of Wind Instruments

SHOSTAKOVICH Symphony No. 15

RACHMANINOFF *The Bells*

HINDEMITH Clarinet Concerto

SIBELIUS Symphony No. 5

BRITTEN Purcell Variations

SHOSTAKOVICH Symphony No. 6

RACHMANINOFF Symphony No. 1

SIBELIUS Symphony No. 6

COMPOSER ENCOUNTERS

Beginning with the 1985–86 season, subscription audiences were invited to hear composers of contemporary works discuss their music on the evening of one of the performances. Composers who have participated in this program are listed here.

1985–86
Stanislaw Skrowaczewski
Richard Wernick
Ellen Taaffe Zwilich
Elliott Carter

1986–87
Bernard Rands
Chinary Ung
Jacob Druckman
Christopher Rouse
Karel Husa
Witold Lutoslawski
Ralph Shapey

1987–88
Lou Harrison
Dominick Argento
Nicholas Thorne
Robert Capanna
Leon Kirchner

1988–1989
Steven Stucky
John Harbison
William Bolcom
Stephen Albert

1989–90
Verna Fine
   (widow of Irving Fine)
John Harbison
Bernard Rands
Mark Kopytman
Milton Babbitt
William Bolcom
Mario Davidovsky
George Rochberg
Joan Tower
George Crumb
Joseph Castaldo

1990–91
Richard Wernick
Jacob Druckman
Shulamit Ran
Daron Hagen
Augusta Read Thomas
Earl Kim
Charles Wuorinen
Bernard Rands

1991–92
Bernard Rands
Stephen Albert
Edwin London
John Duffy
Roberto Sierra
George Perle
George Rochberg

BACKGROUND: THE OPENING PAGE OF RALPH SHAPEY'S SYMPHONIE CONCERTANTE, ONE OF THE ORCHESTRA'S CONSTITUTIONAL COMMISSIONS (1987). REPRINTED WITH PERMISSION OF THEODORE PRESSER CO.

GALAS

Dear Maestro Muti,

Congratulations on your fruitful twenty-year collaboration with The Philadelphia Orchestra. I am so honored to have been included in that wonderful chapter of your musical life. We are all looking forward to the next twenty. ❧ *With love and admiration,*

KATHLEEN BATTLE

Dear Riccardo,

Congratulations on your twenty-year association with The Philadelphia Orchestra. Wishing you all the very best. Hope we will have a chance to make music together very soon. Best wishes.

ITZHAK PERLMAN

TOP: SOPRANO KATHLEEN BATTLE PERFORMED IN THE GALA OPENING CONCERT OF 1984.

CENTER: 9-YEAR-OLD VIOLINIST SARAH CHANG PREPARES FOR HER APPEARANCE AT THE 134TH ACADEMY ANNIVERSARY CONCERT IN 1991.

BOTTOM: SOPRANO RENATA SCOTTO PERFORMS IN THE 128TH ACADEMY ANNIVERSARY CONCERT, 1985

At a press luncheon announcing plans for
Opening Night 1991 are (l. to r.) Alex Pen-
nington, Maestro Muti, MayBelle Rauch,
Schuy Wood, and Cristina Muti.

GALAS CONDUCTED BY RICCARDO MUTI

1981–1982
125th Academy Anniversary Concert
José Carreras, tenor
Rosalind Plowright, soprano

1982–83
Gala Opening Concert
Hildegard Behrens, soprano

1983–84
Gala Opening Concert
Itzhak Perlman, violin

1984–85
Gala Opening Concert
Kathleen Battle, soprano
128th Academy Anniversary Concert
Renata Scotto, soprano
Lando Bartolini, tenor
Eugene Fodor, violin

1985–86
Gala Opening Concert
Isaac Stern, violin

1986–1987
Gala Opening Concert
Singing City Choir

1987–88
Opening Night Concert
Rudolf Serkin, piano
131st Academy Anniversary Concert
Viktoria Mullova, violin
Frederica von Stade, mezzo-soprano

1988–89
Opening Night Concert
Itzhak Perlman, violin

1989–1990
Opening Night Concert
Murray Perahia, piano

1990–91
Opening Night Concert
Yo-Yo Ma, cello
134th Academy Anniversary Concert
Sarah Chang, violin
André Watts, piano
Special Opening Night Performance of
Tosca

1991–92
135th Academy Anniversary Concert
Jessye Norman, soprano
Itzhak Perlman, violin
Special Opening Night Performance of
Pagliacci
Gala Tribute to Riccardo Muti

SUMMERS

The Mann Music Center in Philadelphia's Fairmount Park and the Saratoga Performing Arts Center in Saratoga Springs, New York, present concerts by The Philadelphia Orchestra each summer. For six weeks at the outdoor Philadelphia facility, and three weeks in residence at the New York state festival, the Orchestra plays for thousands of listeners with a variety of conductors and soloists.

In 1990, Charles Dutoit was appointed to the position of Artistic Director and Principal Conductor of the Mann Music Center and Saratoga Performing Arts Center. By unifying the Mann Center and Saratoga seasons for the first time, the organizations and the Orchestra are able to provide continuity of programming and an exciting opportunity to exploit the artistic possibilities of each residency to the fullest.

WITH THE LATE HON. FREDRIC R. MANN AT THE MANN MUSIC CENTER

A BOW AT THE SARATOGA PERFORMING ARTS CENTER

Philadelphia Orchestra:

Rytmiä, draamaa, laulavuutta

Kraft, voima oli Riccardo Mutin ja The Philadelphia -orkesterin tunnussana Paul Hindemithin Es-duuri-sinfonian esityksessä. Kun sinfonian ensiosan alkufanfaari kajahti ilmoille voitokkaan juhlavana ja hurjana, ei ollut enää ~~~~ täkään aihetta ~~~~

MUSIIKKI

Helsin...

Kultur

ember 1987 / Nr. 206

ale Musikfestwochen 1987: 13. Sinfoniekonzert mit Riccardo Muti und dem Philadelphia Orchestra

Freude an der perfekten Ästhetik

katen, die überall in der ~ schaut er uns wie Mona ~ verschleiertem Blick. Auch um bewahrt Riccardo Muti xhaftes, was wiederum in ~ Gegensatz zur Agilität des ~. Ich bin geneigt, das äusse-~ Musizieren zu übertragen: ~it Temperament.

~tagabend hielt – im Jahr der ~hen Musik – das einzige Or-~der Neuen Welt im Kunst-~. Wie die meisten US-En-

~nstagabend, beim 13. Sin-~zert, waren – nach einer ~von fünf Jahren – wieder ~Riccardo M

~ter Allgemeine Zeitung

Gläserne Perfektion

Riccardo Muti und das Philadelphia Orch

„Je preiser einer gekrönt werde, de~ tiefer falle er", soll der ~ Hellmesberger einma~ Auf Riccardo ~ sich h~

M U S I Q U E

SOLEIL

TUTTI PER MUTI!

~t physique avenant, la nouvelle star mondiale de la baguette a ~c Toscanini. A l'occasion de l'ouverture du Festival d'Orc~ ~M.P., un entretien exclusif avec Libération.

l'intégrale de ~ ressenti ce qu~ comme un truis~ de l'orchestra~ bouche à ce su~ **LIBERATION** de publier vo~ et de l~ R.M.— La~ chestration ~ que celle de~ pas rien. ~ l'on pourr~ l'empereur ~ **LIBERAT** nienne de~ être aussi ~ directeur ~ Milan à ~ vos pr~ gorgée~ R.M saints~ ~evre~

LA NACION

Buenos Aires, martes 31 de mayo de 1988

Beethoven a través de

~spiradas v ~

BEYOND
PHILADELPHIA

IN BERLIN'S IMPOSING
PHILHARMONIE, 1984

Performing for new audiences serves artists as much as it does the public. Whether bringing a concert opera to New York or a fresh look at a masterpiece to Los Angeles, Salzburg, Buenos Aires, or Hong Kong, an orchestra refreshes itself. Sometimes, by repeating familiar works in unfamiliar places, the musicians find new depths to the music. With Riccardo Muti, the Orchestra explored new territory, artistically as well as geographically.

During his tenure, they have visited 88 cities in 21 countries on 4 continents. For Maestro Muti, the greatest eye-openers may have been on the tours through the United States, where he encountered not only music lovers, but cultural treasures and natural wonders, from museums in Kansas City, Missouri, and Fort Worth, Texas, to a monastery library in Minnesota, to California's giant redwoods.

Riccardo Muti took no soloists on tour, preferring his orchestra to be the only soloist. Together they filled concert halls across North America and around the world, reaping standing ovations as they went. Among the highlights: performing in Berlin and Paris for the first time since the 1950s; a triumphant London concert that almost didn't happen after a delayed flight; performing in Buenos Aires's historic Teatro Colón and Tokyo's new Suntory Hall; the gridlock in Naples when its native son returned for the first time with his American orchestra; performing in Prague just as Eastern Europe was being loosed from the grip of the Cold War; playing the closing concerts of the 1987 Salzburg Festival, the Orchestra's first appearances in that prestigious festival. The final performances of their last tour together this spring will be, fittingly, the Orchestra's first concerts in Tel Aviv and Jerusalem. Why not end with one more discovery?

THE NEW YORK SEASON

Since 1902, The Philadelphia Orchestra has performed in New York's Carnegie Hall, often presenting its own subscription series there. It also gives occasional concerts on Lincoln Center's Great Performers series at Avery Fisher Hall.

The New York concerts offer a cross-section of instrumental and vocal programs, of familiar and unfamiliar works, enabling New Yorkers to follow The Philadelphia Orchestra on its artistic path, rather than simply to hear an occasional concert on tour. Thus, when John Rockwell wrote in 1985 in *The New York Times,* that "…Riccardo Muti seems to have made a resounding success of his efforts to transform, ever so slowly, one of America's grandest old orchestras into one of America's grandest new ones," he was reflecting on a process that was being closely watched by audiences in his own city, as well as in Philadelphia.

Among the highlights of the New York series were performances of Prokofiev's *Ivan the Terrible* and *Alexander Nevsky,* Verdi's Requiem, two Beethoven piano concertos with the late Claudio Arrau, and Varèse's *Arcana* and Britten's *Four Sea Interludes,* along with Chausson's *Poème de l'amour et de la mer* with Frederica von Stade. There were also collaborations with such outstanding artists as Yehudi Menuhin, Murray Perahia, Jessye Norman, Radu Lupu, Isaac Stern, and the late Malcolm Frager.

For New Yorkers, however, the most outstanding evidence of Riccardo Muti's "transformation" may have been his concert performances of complete operas, which attracted connoisseurs from the world over. Of one, Donal Henahan, then chief music critic of *The New York Times,* wrote, "Mr. Muti and company gave us a *Rigoletto* of such authority, controlled intensity and drive that the memory of all recent staged performances was wiped away." In the following essay, *New York* magazine critic Peter G. Davis further describes the significance of the first concert opera offering, Verdi's *Macbeth,* and those that followed.

Dear Maestro Muti,

This is certainly not a goodbye…but a heartfelt thank you for the 16 years of wondrous music you have made with The Philadelphia Orchestra at Carnegie Hall. 🐾 *The Orchestra itself made its debut at the hall in 1902, and has offered its artistry to a loyal and enthusiastic New York audience for 90 years. But since I came to Carnegie Hall in 1986, it is the Philadelphia Orchestra of Riccardo Muti that I have experienced in some of the most brilliant concerts of recent seasons.* 🐾 *I hope it is not long before we see you here at Carnegie Hall again, and I look forward to future collaborations. For now, all of us here, our Board of Trustees and the Staff, send you our deepest thanks and appreciation for the stellar contribution you have made to Carnegie Hall's tradition of excellence.*

JUDITH ARRON, *Executive Director, Carnegie Hall*

During my years at Carnegie Hall, I have met so many wonderful maestros and each has touched my life with some joy and heartfelt moments; but Maestro Muti, by far, you stand above the rest. You have it all!

DEBBIE KING, *Backstage Attendant, Carnegie Hall*

Lincoln Center for the Performing Arts would like to wish Riccardo Muti all the best as he concludes his final season as Music Director of The Philadelphia Orchestra. Maestro Muti has graced the stage of Avery Fisher Hall on numerous occasions as part of Lincoln Center's Great Performers series. His concerts are full of electricity, innovation, and emotion. We look forward with anticipation to the next stage of his brilliant career.

WILLIAM W. LOCKWOOD, JR., *Executive Producer, Programming, Lincoln Center for the Performing Arts, Inc.*

VIEW FROM NEW YORK

by Peter G. Davis

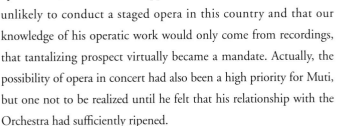

When Riccardo Muti conducted his first concert in Carnegie Hall after becoming Music Director of The Philadelphia Orchestra in 1980, many in the audience must have wondered how this special combination of conductor and orchestra might sound performing an opera. Soon, when it seemed apparent that Muti was unlikely to conduct a staged opera in this country and that our knowledge of his operatic work would only come from recordings, that tantalizing prospect virtually became a mandate. Actually, the possibility of opera in concert had also been a high priority for Muti, but one not to be realized until he felt that his relationship with the Orchestra had sufficiently ripened.

That time came in the fall of 1983, and the conductor decided upon Verdi's *Macbeth* — a surprising choice on the face of it, since the scores from this composer's early period are generally considered showpieces for singers, with the musicians in the pit and the man on the podium supplying a discreet accompaniment. Muti quickly dispelled that narrow-minded notion, demonstrating the powerful effect a great orchestra can make even in the works of Verdi's youth, particularly when a dynamic musical presence is there to shape the performance.

Each aria, duet, and ensemble in *Macbeth* has its own distinctive instrumental character that subtly underscores the drama, through varied rhythmic patterns, ornamental figuration, or simply one plaintive note from a solo woodwind to symbolize a psychological twist in Lady Macbeth's mental deterioration. In Muti's hands, these facets were superbly delineated, generating the musical atmosphere that Verdi intended — unrelentingly dark, threatening, corrosively evil — with unprecedented clarity, precision, and concentrated power, all of it enhanced by the sheer beauty of blended sound that this orchestra produces so naturally.

After such a revelation, opera from Philadelphia would have to be an annual musical event. In the years that followed, Muti offered two additional Verdi works, again from the composer's earlier years: *Rigo-*

letto and *Nabucco*, utilizing the newly prepared critical editions of scores too often taken for granted and marred by carelessly handed-down traditions. Although connoisseurs might have had legitimate complaints about these performances' vocal quality — Verdi singers are scarce the world over — the overall conception and execution showed each opera in a fresh light, recapturing the thrusting vigor and exciting energy that had made both such revolutionary statements a century-and-a-half ago. In a way, it was even salutary to hear the operas, just this once and in this manner, without the trappings of the stage, in order to appreciate their stature as purely *musical* dramas.

Next, after young Verdi, came young Wagner: *The Flying Dutchman* in 1986, an especially interesting project since Muti's approach to this composer was an unknown quantity here, even on records. With a song in each measure backed by an intensely theatrical impulse, the performance struck a fine balance, neither neglecting the music's Italianate lyrical influences nor its Beethovenian symphonic sweep. In *Dutchman*, Muti once again showed himself to be a born opera conductor, one who can clearly perceive the special defining musical characteristics of a score and give them dramatic life. That had also happened in 1984 with an entirely different sort of work, Gluck's *Orfeo ed Euridice*. The conductor preferred the rarely heard Vienna version of 1762 in all its chaste classical simplicity, presenting an interpretation of exceptional poise, dignity, and tonal radiance.

Unfortunately for New Yorkers, Muti's first encounter with Puccini — *Tosca* in 1991 — did not reach Carnegie Hall, but that, as well as *Pagliacci* in 1992 with Luciano Pavarotti, will eventually be available on records. These seven works only represent a small sampling of Muti's repertory, but each performance in itself remains a precious memory: the rare operatic partnership between a great symphony orchestra and a great conductor.

Peter G. Davis *is the music critic for* New York *magazine.*

VIEW FROM LOS ANGELES

by Martin Bernheimer

Los Angeles, believe it or not, is a reasonably sophisticated city. Amid the palm trees and the glitz one can find a major symphony orchestra, and several minor ones too. When important ensembles from the other coast or from Europe take to touring, this city usually figures prominently in the itinerary. We are spoiled at worst, jaded at best. Sooner or later, everyone comes here. Still, we recognize something special when we encounter it. The Southern California visits by Riccardo Muti and The Philadelphia Orchestra have been special.

When we first saw the dashing young maestro on what we thought was Eugene Ormandy's podium, we tended to be a little skeptical. We worried that the Italian firebrand might not sustain the mellow romantic ideals of his popular predecessor. We fretted about possible destruction of the lush Philadelphia sound—a unique sound predicated on suave phraseology in depth, with the central focus on silken-string cantabile.

The worrying and fretting turned out to be silly. Muti obviously savored the finest attributes of the Philadelphia sound that he inherited, but he used those attributes to create something of deeper value. Never interested in easy effects or in surface sheen for its own sake, he probed for subtle nuance and expressive logic. Never content with traditional evasions, he tried valiantly—and often successfully—to return to basics: the composer's intentions, explicit in the score and implicit in the style.

Muti is a virtuoso technician. For him technique is just a beginning, however. Precision cannot preclude passion. Muti also happens to be an extraordinary scholar and something of a stylist. He likes to examine the music that he performs within a specific historical, artistic, and sociological context. He cares about the impact of period and place.

A few special memories:

🎜 A *Symphonie fantastique* in which the impact of Berlioz's rhetorical indulgence was enhanced, for a change, by understatement. Muti's performance was straight and taut, clean and lean. It moved in one long, arching breath. For all its surging drama, it was elegant.

🎜 A Beethoven Fifth in which the introductory *Allegro con brio* bristled with impetuous fury. The momentum never Xagged, yet it never seemed forced. The inherent "Sturm und Drang" reXected urgency, not frenzy.

🎜 Three trifles by Giuseppe Martucci (1856-1909) in which Muti somehow elevated neo-Neapolitan kitsch to high art.

Most illuminating, perhaps, was a 1989 program in a multi-million-dollar emporium in Orange County. We had feared that the new cultural center suffered from, chronic if not terminal, acoustical mush. Muti and the Philadelphians proved that there are no such things as hopeless halls, just indifferent conductors and inferior orchestras.

They stripped the sentimental gush from Tchaikovsky's *Romeo and Juliet* and exposed honest pathos in the process. Although they couldn't do much to vitalize Vincent Persichetti's Fifth Symphony, which followed, they still earned admiration for paying attention to a neglected contemporary cause. Finally, they turned to Prokofiev's music for Shakespeare's "star-cross'd lovers" and brought dapper charm to the lighter moments, jaunty flamboyance to the episodes of grotesquerie, brutal force to the heroic climaxes, and exquisite serenity to the love music.

The audience responded to the tragic catharsis of the Tomb Scene with the ultimate tribute: stunned silence. For a long time, no one dared breathe. Then came release and a thunderous ovation. It was a typical Muti triumph.

Modern conductors tend to be cool, dull, and objective (if there is such a thing) at one extreme, or hot, flashy, and insensitive at the other. Muti remains a stubborn poet in an unpoetic age. He is a thinking person's maestro.

MARTIN BERNHEIMER *is the music critic for the* Los Angeles Times.

CIGNA Chairman and CEO
Wilson Taylor and Mrs. Taylor enjoy a relaxed moment
with the Mutis.

A performance in Chicago,
during the 50th Anniversary
North American Tour, 1986

We at the Kennedy Center began experiencing the miracle of Riccardo Muti and The Philadelphia Orchestra in 1973, when our Concert Hall was barely two years old. We have since then treasured them immensely and cheered them often. I am overjoyed that, as Maestro Muti assumes his new position of Laureate Conductor, we do not have to bid him and the Philadelphians farewell on this occasion, but can look forward to many more glorious years of magnificent music-making in our Concert Hall. JAMES D. WOLFENSOHN, *Chairman, The John F. Kennedy Center for the Performing Arts*

Dear Maestro Muti,
You have served as an extraordinary ambassador for The Philadelphia Orchestra and our city. Beyond the nine international tours on which you have taken the Orchestra, its series of radio broadcasts, produced by Chicago's WFMT, has enlightened and moved millions of listeners in the United States, Europe, and Asia. ❦ CIGNA is proud to have helped support concerts that have brought the excitement of live performances by a world-class orchestra to millions of devoted listeners. Barbara and I are particularly appreciative of the opportunities we've had to travel with you and to share the excitement of these events. ❦ Thank you, Maestro, for your extraordinary artistic excellence, your energy, and your generous enthusiasm in reaching out to people throughout the world. WILSON H. TAYLOR, *Chairman and Chief Executive Officer, CIGNA Corporation*

Dear Maestro Muti,
ARCO Chemical has now hosted concerts during the last two European tours of The Philadelphia Orchestra. From both a personal aesthetic and a "corporate" satisfaction standpoint, these concerts have been high points of my European experience. Wishes for all the best at La Scala and looking forward to many future appearances in Philadelphia. ALAN R. HIRSIG, *President and Chief Executive Officer, ARCO Chemical Company*

TEATRO ALLA SCALA

ENTE AUTONOMO

Rappr. N. **229**   FUORI ABBONAMENTO

GIOVEDI 3 SETTEMBRE 1987 - ORE 20

CONCERTO STRAORDINARIO

THE PHILADELPHIA ORCHESTRA

DIRETTORE

RICCARDO MUTI

PROGRAMMA

PAUL HINDEMITH   SINFONIA IN MI BEM. MAGG.
Sehr lebhaft - Lebhafter
Sehr langsam
Lebhaft - Ein wenig ruhiger - Im früheren Zeitmass
Mässig schnelle Halbe - Intermezzo, im gleichen Zeitmass
Wie zuerst - Breit bewegt - Lebhaft mit höchster Kraft

HECTOR BERLIOZ   SYMPHONIE FANTASTIQUE op. 14
Rêveries - Passions (Largo - Allegro agitato e appassionato assai)
Un bal (Valse. Allegro non troppo)
Scène au champs (Adagio)
Marche au supplice (Allegretto non troppo)
Songe d'une nuit du sabbat (Larghetto - Allegro)

PREZZI (Tasse comprese)

Poltrona di platea L. **39.000** - Poltroncina di platea L. **32.000**

Posto in palco L. **32.000** - Ingresso supplementare ai palchi L. **16.000**

Posto numerato Iª galleria L. **14.000** - Posto numerato IIª galleria L. **10.000** - Ingresso L. **3.000**

Sui biglietti dei posti riservati o acquistati nei giorni precedenti quello del concerto si applica il 10% di servizio prenotazione.

Informazioni alla biglietteria del Teatro: tel. 807041 (4 linee urbane); nastro registrato continuo 24 ore.

Prenotazioni telefoniche alla biglietteria del Teatro: 809126 (3 linee urbane); orario tutti i giorni dalle 10 alle 12,30 (sabato e domenica escluso)

IMPAGINAZIONE E STAMPA ARTI GRAFICHE CONFALONIERI - MILANO

TOURS CONDUCTED BY RICCARDO MUTI

1980-81

Far East Tour: conducts 7 concerts in Japan

1981-82

European Tour: 14 concerts in 8 cities, including Orchestra's first appearances in Berlin since 1955, in Paris since 1958, and first appearances at the Edinburgh Festival. Appearances in Vienna, Lucerne, Frankfurt, Brussels, London

1982-83

United States Tour: concerts in 11 cities, including Chicago, Minneapolis, Ann Arbor, Bloomington, Nashville

1983-84

European Tour: 14 concerts in 11 cities, including Orchestra's first concerts at Vienna Festival, Paris International Festival, in Naples and at La Scala, Milan

1984-85

West Coast Tour: concerts in San Francisco, Pasadena, Tempe. Includes taping of Berlioz's *Symphonie fantastique* for national television broadcast

Far East Tour: 13 concerts in Japan and Korea, and Orchestra's first appearance in Hong Kong

1985-86

50th Anniversary North American Tour: 16 cities in U.S. and Canada, celebrating 50th anniversary of Orchestra cross-country touring, and representing U.S.A. at Vancouver's Expo '86

1986-87

Pennyslvania Tour: 4 cities in Pennsylvania and Columbus, Ohio

European Tour: 13 concerts in 9 cities, including Orchestra's first appearances in Salzburg, closing Salzburg Festival; its first

concerts in Helsinki under Riccardo Muti; appearances at Lucerne Festival and Milan's La Scala; and television broadcast in Frankfurt. Concerts in Munich, Amsterdam, Berlin, Paris

1987-88

Tour of the Americas: 5 concerts in southwestern United States, and two weeks in South America under auspices of United States Information Agency; Orchestra's first visits to that continent in 22 years. Concerts in Caracas, São Paulo, Buenos Aires, Rio de Janeiro

1988-89

Tour of California and Japan: performances in San Francisco, Pasadena, Costa Mesa, and 9 concerts in Japan, including 4 in Tokyo

1989-90

Transcontinental Tour: conducts concerts in Toronto, New Haven, Hartford, Pittsburgh, Ames, Lincoln, Cleveland, Seattle, Eugene, San Francisco

1990-91

European Tour: 13 concerts in 11 cities, including Orchestra's first appearances in Prague and Bologna, and its first performance in Geneva since 1955. Concerts in Amsterdam, Frankfurt, Hamburg, Munich, Vienna, Florence, Milan, Paris

1991-92

European Tour: includes first Orchestra performances in Tel Aviv and Jerusalem, at Expo '92 in Seville, and in Ravenna. Concerts in Barcelona, Madrid, Genoa, Vienna, London, Brussels

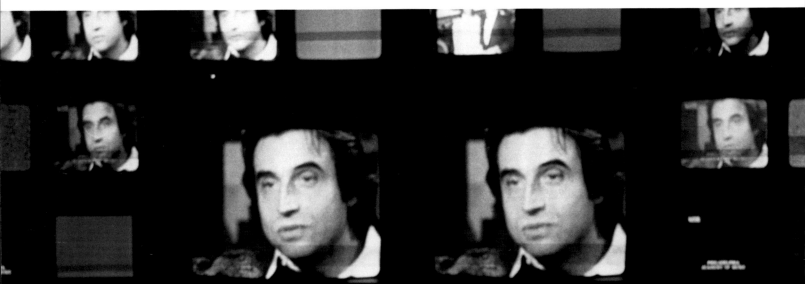

TOWARD A
BROADER COMMUNITY

SHARING THOUGHTS WITH "KID REPORTERS" AT A PRESS CONFERENCE IN HIS OFFICE ORGANIZED BY THE *PHILADELPHIA DAILY NEWS*, 1985

Early in his tenure, Riccardo Muti was asked to provide testimony to the Pennsylvania State Board of Education, which was considering a reduction in requirements for music and art in the schools. He responded with the following statement, which was reprinted later in a *Philadelphia Inquirer* editorial:

"Music is more than a hobby, an entertainment or a pastime for the elite. It is part of the soul of every human being. Music speaks to us in a way that words cannot, to our feelings as well as our thoughts.

"Throughout history, men and governments have recognized this power of music and the other arts and have tried to control them. Restriction of artistic freedom is unfortunately one of the most potent weapons some governments still use today.

"That is why a free country has a special responsibility to nourish this vital aspect of its culture. By giving children and adults the opportunity to develop their understanding of the language of music and their sensitivity to it, we reinforce the ideals of democracy and freedom.

"If we choose, however, to push music aside and to neglect its development in our youth, we are doing more than denying a privilege. We are stunting the spirit, and that is nothing short of barbaric."

Through open rehearsals, national and international radio broadcasts, and televised concerts in which he gave spoken introductions to each work, Maestro Muti sought to bring the language of music to as many as wished to listen. He initiated Opera Week, a series of discussion/demonstrations with other opera experts, and often opened his final rehearsals to the public, inviting the audience to join him and the Orchestra in their exploration of opera. A special free concert for new listeners led to the annual "Come and Meet the Music" programs, featuring spoken introductions by the conductor and now often televised by KYW-TV3.

Over 150 secondary schools from Pennsylvania, Southern New Jersey, and Delaware have attended his dress rehearsals, which he opened to students in his second season as Music Director. He worked with young musicians at The Curtis Institute of Music and Westminster Choir College, and with musicologists at the University of Pennsylvania. In his free time he joined Orchestra musicians in their support of causes that affect us all: raising money for the homeless and for nuclear disarmament efforts.

Recognizing his commitment to learning at all levels, several colleges and universities have awarded Riccardo Muti honorary doctorate degrees. In 1987, when the University of Pennsylvania also asked him to give the commencement address, some business students were quoted as wondering what someone from so specialized a field could offer such a broad range of graduates. They needn't have worried. His speech, focusing on the arts as a catalyst for approaching issues and affirming values, elicited a standing ovation from the graduates and the entire assembly in Franklin Field, some 25,000 strong.

TOP: A GROUP OF STUDENTS FROM OVERBROOK HIGH SCHOOL HAVE A VISIT BACKSTAGE WHILE ATTENDING A DRESS REHEARSAL, 1991. OVER 215 SCHOOLS HAVE PARTICIPATED IN THE PROGRAM SINCE MAESTRO MUTI OPENED THE REHEARSALS TO HIGH SCHOOL AND COLLEGE STUDENTS IN 1981.

BOTTOM: MAKING ONE OF HIS PERIODIC VISITS UP LOCUST STREET TO WORK WITH THE STUDENT ORCHESTRA OF THE CURTIS INSTITUTE OF MUSIC, 1990

Dear Maestro Muti,

I write to thank you for your commitment to, and support of, music education for people of all ages. ❧ *Thank you, too, for opening dress rehearsals to area students, as these are unique opportunities to watch and hear a work in progress. Such experiences are invaluable in breaking down the invisible walls which seem to exist between the stage and the auditorium and surround classical music. Most attending students had never before been inside the Academy of Music — much less heard an orchestra perform.* ❧ *I remember well the day you flew backstage between concert opera rehearsals and stopped briefly to witness thirty children, aged nine and ten, ready to go on stage to read stories with musicians from the Orchestra. You stopped, stared at them, they stared at you, and your face broke into a radiant smile that left a lasting impression on the students. "Was that really Maestro Muti?" they asked later. When told it was, the reply was "Wow!"* ❧ *Please know you have made a lasting contribution to thousands of young people over many years.*
PHYLLIS BEESON SUSEN, *Director of Education,*
The Philadelphia Orchestra Association

Attending the September 23 rehearsal was a diversified group of students — our freshman and sophomore music majors as well as international students from Japan, Mexico, Venezuela, El Salvador, Jordan, and the Dominican Republic. As always, we were thrilled and impressed by the Orchestra's excellence and by your sensitivity to both overall effect and details of nuance. Thank you for reaching out to young people through the Orchestra.
SR. KATHLEEN C. DOUTT, *Associate Professor of Music,*
Immaculata College, 1988

Dear Maestro,

All Philadelphia has been enriched by your presence; we at Curtis are particularly appreciative of your interest in, and encouragement of, our students. We all thank you for your generosity, for your enthusiasm, and particularly for your magnificent music-making. ❧ *We wish you the greatest joy and fulfillment in your life ahead.* ❧ *On behalf of The Curtis Institute of Music,*
GARY GRAFFMAN, *Director, The Curtis Institute of Music*

Dear Maestro Muti,
*I want to tell you how much I have learned from you while rehearsing
and performing this year and last year. You have inspired me and challenged me to set ever higher goals for myself, to reach for the essence of
every piece of music, and to develop my ability to listen even more deeply.*
KIRIN NIELSEN, *student at Westminster Choir College, 1988*

Dear Maestro,
*On behalf of the American Symphony Orchestra League, I have the
pleasure of sending congratulations and warm good wishes as you and
The Philadelphia Orchestra celebrate twenty years of collaboration with
music.* ❧ *This occasion gives the League an opportunity to thank you
for your very special efforts in helping us to develop a new generation of
American talent. Your participation in our conducting workshop, held
at the Curtis Institute several years ago, will long be remembered and
appreciated, not only by the young conductors selected for your master
class, but also by all who were there to observe and talk with you in the
discussion that followed.* ❧ *We recall that you asked the Curtis Orchestra not to rehearse the repertoire for the master class so that the skill of*

*each conductor would be tested from the downbeat. We can still hear
the sound of the orchestra when you yourself introduced them to the
Vespri overture.* ❧ *In just a few hours on that Sunday afternoon, we
shared some of what The Philadelphia Orchestra has experienced now
for two decades. We at the League, our member orchestras, and countless musicians, young and old, are happy to join in this celebration of
your leadership. We thank you for sharing your music with all of us.*
CATHERINE FRENCH, *Chief Executive Officer,*
American Symphony Orchestra League

Dear Maestro Muti,
*The performance of The Philadelphia Orchestra on live TV last evening,
under your direction, was a masterpiece. I viewed your performance with
such enthusiasm, that at the conclusion of the Boléro, I rose from my easy
chair and gave you and the Orchestra a standing ovation.* ❧ *Your com-
ments were sincere and touched all of us — truly the mark of a great
artist in the mold of men such as Michelangelo and Toscanini.*
PETER W. RADICE, JR., *Princeton, NJ, 1989*

Dear Maestro,

The entire staff of KYW-TV3 joins me in wishing you continued success on this special occasion of well-deserved tribute. It has been a privilege to have collaborated with you in bringing the great sound of The Philadelphia Orchestra into Delaware Valley homes through our live telecasts of the "Come and Meet the Music" series. It should give you great satisfaction to know that your efforts made it possible to bring the Orchestra and the great composers to a whole new audience through television.

JONATHAN KLEIN, *Vice President and General Manager, KYW-TV3*

Dear Maestro Muti,

Over the years, and especially recently, WFLN has been an ardent supporter/ally of the Orchestra's endeavors. We are delighted to work closely with an organization whose work represents the highest in musical achievement, and we thank you for your contribution to that effort. Personally, among the many highlights during your tenure as Music Director, the concert operas under your direction are among the most moving concert experiences I have ever had. On behalf of WFLN, I wish you continued success and look forward to your periodic returns. Buona fortuna!

RICHARD TEDESCO, *Vice President & General Manager, WFLN*

Dear Maestro Muti,

All of us at WHYY-TV12 and 91FM, the public broadcasting stations serving the Delaware Valley, wish you continued success as you leave your post as Music Director of The Philadelphia Orchestra. Your years in Philadelphia have been extraordinarily fruitful and joyful. You have continued a grand musical tradition and have fine-tuned it with your genius. ❧ WHYY and the Orchestra have enjoyed a close association during your tenure. It began with TV12's five-part series "The Fabulous Philadelphians: From Ormandy to Muti." It continued on 91FM with simulcasts of the Orchestra in concert and most recently with an in-depth, three-part interview with you on "Artscape." ❧ You have enriched Philadelphia with your musical brilliance. All of us are richer for it, and, thankfully, we'll still be able to be blessed with your musical legacy.

FREDERICK BREITENFELD, JR., *President, WHYY-TV12 and 91FM*

TOP: On behalf of the musicians and staff of The Philadelphia Orchestra Association, Maestro Muti presents a check to Pennsylvania Ballet Artistic Director Christopher d'Amboise, for its successful "Save the Ballet" campaign, 1991.

BOTTOM: Audience enthusiasm during the Orchestra Week concert carried over to the throng of backstage visitors, 1985.

RIGHT: Orchestra members draw from thousands of entries during *It's Your Orchestra Week* contest in 1985. Winners attended a free concert in the Academy of Music conducted by Maestro Muti, broadcast live on WIOQ-FM. He gave spoken introductions for the benefit of the many who had previously not attended an Orchestra concert.

During one of the few associations I've had with Maestro Muti, I was most impressed by his commitment to the welfare of artists in all disputes, not only within his own orchestra. In March of 1991, when the Pennsylvania Ballet was in dire need of support, Riccardo and The Philadelphia Orchestra led an effort that raised 15,000 precious dollars to help "Save The Ballet." That generous, externally minded spirit inspired us all when we needed it most.

CHRISTOPHER D'AMBOISE, *President and Artistic Director, Pennsylvania Ballet*

Settlement Music School was proud to welcome Maestro Muti to Philadelphia in 1982 with a gala concert at Penn's Landing. The concert was performed by members of The Philadelphia Orchestra who were former students of the School, and was a demonstration of the connection of the Orchestra to the community and to Settlement. We know that Mr. Muti's impact on our city will last beyond his tenure as Music Director, and we applaud his musicianship and his many artistic achievements.

ROBERT CAPANNA, *Executive Director, Settlement Music School*

Dear Maestro,

One of my first memories from the time I joined the Orchestra in 1982 is hearing you say, "My door is always open." ❧ In 1987, after a rehearsal in Carnegie Hall, I explained how Philadelphia's problem with homelessness was getting worse. We talked about my plan to give a benefit concert with the Academy Chamber Players called HOME-AID that would raise money for organizations that help homeless people. You listened with great intensity and immediately agreed to add your name to the advisory board. Over the next three years you helped us in many ways, and, finally, agreed to conduct HOME-AID 3. ❧ It was one of the few times your schedule permitted you to conduct outside the Academy, and the conditions (lighting and space constraints) were less than perfect. During the rehearsal at St. Mark's Church, it seemed like a new spirit had come over all of us—we all came together to share some part of ourselves, not just as musicians, but as human beings. Thanks for the joy you bring to music-making, your concern for others, and your friendship.

BARBARA GOVATOS, *Violin, The Philadelphia Orchestra*

During the autumn of 1982, a group of Philadelphia Orchestra musicians met with Maestro Muti to propose an idea for a gala concert benefitting organizations dedicated to halting the nuclear arms race. Without the slightest hesitation or consultation with anyone, Maestro Muti gave us an emphatic YES. When we thanked him, his response was that it was he who wanted to thank us for asking him. "This is my planet too....we are all citizens of the same world," he said. ❧ His musical directorship of three Concerts for Humanity (1983, 1984, 1988) spoke positively through the universal language of music for the triumph of humanity's spirit over violence and added a sense of legitimacy

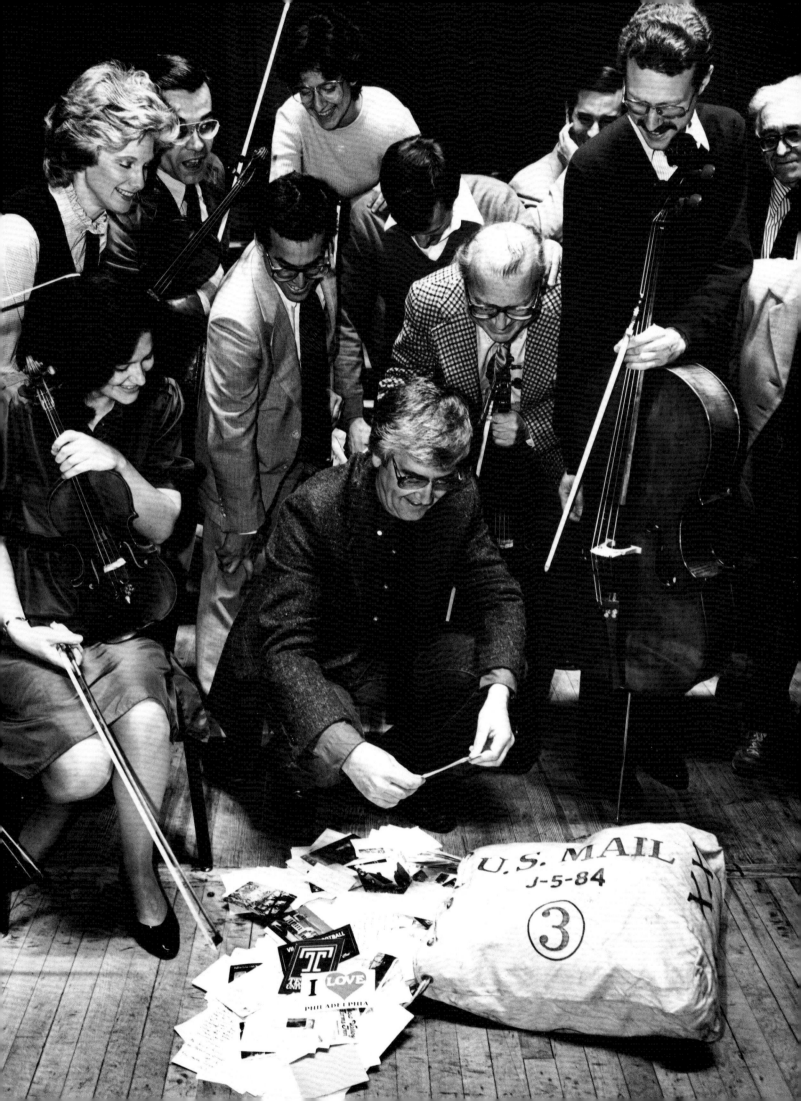

with dignity to the disarmament cause. Hundreds of musicians from The Philadelphia Orchestra, free-lance community, and Choral Arts Society along with numerous support personnel jumped at the chance to donate their services along with Riccardo Muti. His presence attracted soloists André Watts, Emanuel Ax, Wilhelmenia Fernandez, and Malcolm Frager along with world-renowned speakers, bringing audiences together from all social, economic, and political back-grounds. The concerts were spine-tingling. ❧ In addition to raising money for work locally and nationally, these concerts helped unite many separate peace groups in Philadelphia into one, effective voice. That group, Professional Organizations for Nuclear Arms Control (an organization of concerned business executives, educators, lawyers, musicians, nurses, physicians, and, later, psychologists), has become the model for similar groups in other major cities. We owe Maestro Riccardo Muti tremendous gratitude for making our dream a reality as he courageously stood on the side of global harmony.

RANDY GARDNER, *Philadelphia Orchestra horn, and Past President, Musicians for Nuclear Responsibility*

Riccardo Muti non aveva ancora compiuto 27 anni quando, nel 1968, gli affidai la direzione stabile dell'Orchestra del Teatro Comunale e del Maggio Musicale di Firenze. Non aveva ancora diretto un'opera del grande repertorio: ma era già Riccardo Muti. Con tutte le qualità artistiche ed umane che gli vengono universalmente riconosciute. ❧ Dopo aver conquistato all'istante l'orchestra, conquistò fulmineamente il pubblico. Senza concedere nulla. Otteneva il massimo effetto senza indulgere mai alla ricerca di effetti. Coglieva trionfi senza dare mai l'impressione di cercare il successo. Più che al pubblico sembrava pensare solo a servire la Musica che faceva rivivere e che offriva agli ascoltatori. Impegnava tutto se stesso non per

Riccardo Muti was not yet 27 years old when, in 1968, he was entrusted with the musical direction of the Orchestra del Teatro Comunale and of the Maggio Musicale in Florence. He had not yet conducted an opera from the standard repertoire, but he was already Riccardo Muti. With all the artistic and human qualities for which he has become recognized around the world. ❧ After having won over the orchestra from the beginning, he conquered the audience in a flash. Without making any concessions. He achieved the maximum impact without ever indulging in superficial effects. He accumulated triumphs without ever giving the impression of seeking success. Rather, to the audience he seemed to be solely concerned with serving the music, which he brought to life and offered to the listeners. He engaged his entire being not to create "his" interpretations, but to carry out the intentions of the composer. Controlling each note so that he could later abandon himself to each phrase. With freedom along with rigor. Scrupulously obeying each written sign so as to interpret that which cannot be written with words. Totally dominating the orchestra through an unconditional ascendant and prestige. Knowing how to be amicably close to each player yet maintain, at the same time, the appropriate respectful distance. With the result that the orchestra and soloists are inspired to give their utmost, and that the music receives the maximum expressive intensity. Without ever going over the line. Giving almost the impression of the unattainable. ❧ Today Muti's qualities appear augmented by experience that goes beyond the routine, and by a maturity that has left intact freshness, enthusiasm and youthful spontaneity. That is why success has not damaged, but on the contrary has virtually deepened, his human qualities stamped with absolute rectitude, deep morality, and a luminous rapport with every other human being.
ROMAN VLAD

dare interpretazioni "sue", ma per realizzare le intenzioni dell'autore. Con intuito pari alla comprensione razionale. Controllando ogni nota per potersi poi abbandonare ad ogni frase. Con libertà pari al rigore. Eseguendo con scrupolo ogni segno scritto per poter interpretare ciò che non si puo scrivere. Dominando totalmente l'orchestra grazie ad un prestigio e ad un ascendente incondizionati. Sapendo essere amichevolmente vicino ad ogni singolo suonatore pur serbando, nel contempo, le dovute distanze. Col risultato di portare l'orchestra ed i solisti a dare il meglio delle loro possibilità e di conferire alle musiche interpretate la massima intensità espressiva. Senza mai strafare. Dando quasi la misura dell'incommensurabile. ❧ Oggi le qualità di Muti appaiono esaltate da un'esperienza che trascende ogni routine e da una maturazione che lascia intatte freschezza, slancio e spontaneità giovanili. Così come il successo non ha scalfito, ma semmai ha virtualmente approfondito, le sue qualita umane improntate ad assoluta rettitudine, a profonda moralità, ad un luminoso rapporto col prossimo.
ROMAN VLAD

Dear Maestro Muti,

Six years ago, when you delivered the Westminster Choir College Commencement address, you told our students, "To be good musicians, we must go into the music always more deeply." ❧ Sharing that experience — going inside the music with one of the great musicians of our time — has changed the musical lives of countless Westminster Choir College students. You have been their source of inspiration and teacher at the highest level. As they take their places as professional musicians, our graduates will forever use the knowledge gained from performing the world's great choral music with you. ❧ Westminster Choir College is honored to have had the opportunity to award you the degree Doctor of Music, honoris causa, in recognition of the contributions you have made to the world of music and to our students. We will always cherish the time you have spent on our campus and making music with us. ❧ All of us at Westminster Choir College wish you continued success. We look forward to performing with you in the future.
WILLIAM D. MCGARRY, Chief Executive Officer, Westminster Choir College

Dear Maestro Muti,

Philadelphia gratefully acknowledges that it owes its place on the international musical map to the vision and inspiration of three great men who have guided the Orchestra through our century: Leopold Stokowski, Eugene Ormandy, and Riccardo Muti. Philadelphians — native and adopted — speak these names with pride and affection. Maestro Muti, when we look back on your twenty-year association with our city, we feel privileged and honored to have benefitted from your considerable talents and humanity. ❧ The University of Pennsylvania is particularly proud to count you as one of our own by virtue of the honorary degree you hold from Penn. It is truly heartfelt, then, as in the best university tradition we wish you Godspeed.
SHELDON HACKNEY, President, University of Pennsylvania

Dear Maestro Muti,

Word of your impending departure as Music Director of The Philadelphia Orchestra has given us pause to remember with great happiness the occasion of your visit to Mount Holyoke College in 1986. The citation read here when you received the degree of Doctor of Music noted:
"As a student whose attention was engaged by studies in philosophy, as well as in music, you earned degrees in both disciplines and have demonstrated in your performances a profound respect for the scholarship that illuminates a composer's intentions. Your performances bring the finest in music-making to ever-widening audiences, and your life of dedication to artistic ideals and unqualified excellence serves as an inspiration to young musicians around the world."

❧ Those words, perhaps even more apt today than in 1986, are worth repeating as you celebrate your years with The Philadelphia Orchestra. Mount Holyoke is proud indeed to count you among its honorary graduates.
ELIZABETH T. KENNAN, President, Mount Holyoke College

You leave the Curtis Institute as a fine player, or composer, or conductor, or whatever your medium is. But that is only a part of what the world expects of you. You leave with something else, something more important, and that is the obligation through music to help society become better.
RICCARDO MUTI, *Commencement Address,*
The Curtis Institute of Music, 1991

To be receptive is to be willing to experience something fully, without prejudgments. The arts offer a way for people to exercise this quality, to nourish it so that it can remain with them. I hear so often from people about why they don't come to concerts. They say, "I don't understand the music." I tell them that nobody understands, really. What we are all trying to do is bring ourselves as deeply as possible into the emotions of a composer, into whatever it was that compelled him to write the music. We cannot do this with our minds — only by opening our souls.
RICCARDO MUTI, *Commencement Address,*
University of Pennsylvania, 1987

ABOVE: GREETING GRADUATES AT
THE CURTIS INSTITUTE OF MUSIC
AFTER BEING AWARDED AN HON-
ORARY DOCTORATE OF MUSIC AND
GIVING THE COMMENCEMENT
ADDRESS, 1991

LEFT: SPEAKING TO THE 231ST
GRADUATING CLASS OF THE UNI-
VERSITY OF PENNSYLANIA, AT
FRANKLIN FIELD, 1987. MAESTRO
MUTI WAS AWARDED AN HON-
ORARY DOCTORATE OF MUSIC.

RIGHT: RECEIVING AN HONORARY
DOCTORATE OF PHILOSOPHY IN
1991 FROM THE UNIVERSITY OF
BOLOGNA, THE WORLD'S OLDEST
UNIVERSITY.

EXTENDED FAMILY

RICCARDO AND CRISTINA MUTI
WITH THEIR THREE CHILDREN,
CHIARA, FRANCESCO, AND
DOMENICO NEAR THEIR HOME IN
RAVENNA, ITALY

A WORKING FRIENDSHIP

by Judith Karp Kurnick

It has been thirteen years since my first encounter with Riccardo Muti, as a journalist interviewing him for a French music magazine. Dressed in an impeccable suit, he carried himself with an old-world formality that implied the utmost gravity and, I imagined, possibly self-importance. Yet as he conversed in a second language with wit and effortless grace, Muti's bearing lost its severity. Full of boundless curiosity about this country and its culture, he was as pleased to ask questions as he was to answer those about himself, and he listened with complete attention.

At the same time he displayed principles that were clearly well-formed and well-tested, and the testing of them had given him a piercing comprehension of human nature. I saw that he was not afraid to fight for his beliefs, but that he rarely would need to. It's difficult to resist a born leader.

Some musicians in The Philadelphia Orchestra say they knew, from the first time he conducted them in 1972 at the age of 31, that he would be their next Music Director. (One told him so at the time, and encountered another quality, modesty, in his sincere dismissal of the idea.) Others delighted in the sheer physicality that seemed to flow from Muti's Neapolitan tradition, by which a mimed gesture or a facial expression communicated images far more powerful than words. Certainly all respected the authority that asserted itself without effort, and that respect was returned to them. Musicians much older than he in years found themselves looking to this man for wisdom.

Over the years, I, too, came to value and trust his opinion as I would that of a close relative. And I feel immensely fortunate to be able to count him, and Cristina as I have come to know her, as friends. Because the Mutis do not take friendship lightly.

In that first interview I learned that he was not a person who did *anything* lightly. And when I joined the Orchestra staff a few years later, I realized that, with Muti, there was no such thing as "business as usual." For him each work of music was a treasure to be pursued. He dove into the world of its composer and his time with a passion, doing everything possible to carry the musicians with him, and anyone else who happened to be in his path. He speaks of how every performance should be an "event;" the truth is, for Muti, every *moment* is an event.

He holds those around him to the same standards. Indeed, his greatest disappointment in people, whether in meetings, rehearsals, press conferences, performances, or walking in the street, is when they do not seem to *feel* anything. It is almost as if they are hurting him personally.

Much has been said about Riccardo Muti's attributes by the many who have contributed to this book. What is not often appreciated, however, is the effort he expends every day to maintain that delicate balance of principle, preparation, and humanity in the face of a life that is packed with schedules and responsibilities. The hundreds of times he turns down invitations of all kinds in order to study. The fierce commitment to his family that has caused him to travel hundreds of miles for a day at home in Ravenna, before his next engagement. The insistence on carving out a few hours of rest prior to each and every concert in order to give his best. And above all, the reliance on friends and "extended family," to share a joke or a story, a meal or a telephone call, to commiserate on the problems and exult in the triumphs.

Many Philadelphians probably will not realize the full extent of what Riccardo Muti has given them until long after he has gone.

JUDITH KARP KURNICK *is a writer and public relations consultant who served as The Philadelphia Orchestra's Director of Public Relations from 1983–89.*

THE PHILADELPHIA ORCHESTRA

Dear Maestro Muti,
On the occasion of this tribute honoring you and your contributions to the life and legends of The Philadelphia Orchestra, we would like to convey, on behalf of all your friends and colleagues in the Orchestra, our best wishes for happiness and success in both your personal and artistic life in the years ahead. ❧ *Twelve years are not enough to explore more than a fraction of the great music in which you excel. Nonetheless, you have given us a wealth of musical memories to cherish, and we thank you for challenging us to give our best.* ❧ *Although your Music Directorship with this orchestra is now drawing to an end, we look forward to our continuing musical collaboration with you as Laureate Conductor.*
ALBERT FILOSA, *Chairman;* MARK GIGLIOTTI, MORRIS SHULIK, ROBERT KESSELMAN, SANG-MIN PARK, *The Orchestra Musicians' Committee*

Dear Maestro Muti,
Your years as Music Director have been rewarding experiences for me, both professionally and personally. Under your direction, I feel I have further developed as a musician, and I am deeply grateful for the understanding and kindness you have extended to me. I consider your departure from the Orchestra a great personal loss. I wish to convey to you my very best wishes.
DAVID ARBEN, *Associate Concertmaster*

I am probably one of the few members of the Orchestra who can say he was hired by two of its Music Directors: first by Mr. Ormandy in 1968 and the second time by Maestro Muti as Principal after I came back to The Philadelphia Orchestra from my tenure as conductor in South America. ❧ *Maestro Muti fulfilled one of my dreams in life when, after*

RICCARDO MUTI CONDUCTING THE PHILADELPHIA ORCHESTRA, 1990

I played for him and the audition committee, he made me one of the principals of this Orchestra. That was one of my dreams when I came to this country as an immigrant. His programming of Gluck, Mozart, Beethoven so often during all these years gave a new challenge to the position of first chair players, because of his demanding perfectionism at rehearsals and concerts. ❧ *Maestro Muti has been always an inspiration to my musical knowledge as a violinist and as a conductor. He has enriched my artistic life with great memories of so many wonderful performances. I am proud to have been part of this orchestra during his recordings of so many works, in particular his cycle of Beethoven's symphonies. I am glad he will continue to be with us as Laureate Conductor.*
LUIS BIAVA, *Principal Second Violin*

Dear Riccardo,
Congratulations on your twenty-year affiliation with The Philadelphia Orchestra. Appreciation and thanks must go to you for bringing our orchestra to the world-class stature we now have. I believe special praise must go to Cristina for the sacrifices she has made in sharing you with us for all these years. I will always have fond memories of our friendship and music-making and hope it continues for many years to come. Elinor joins me in wishing you and your family our very best in the future.
NORMAN CAROL, *Concertmaster*

CONFERRING WITH CONCERTMASTER NORMAN CAROL DURING A RECORDING SESSION, 1984

When Riccardo Muti became the conductor of The Philadelphia Orchestra, my life essentially changed. Since music — performing it, listening to it, and thinking about it — has always been an all-encompassing part of me, his presence produced a feeling of renewal, rebirth — a renaissance of sensitivity and understanding toward my playing and the playing of others almost comparable to discovering clearer, purer vision. ❧ *He brings with him the ancient civilization of the Mediterranean with its culture, literature, history, warmth, and humanity. He brings the value of his thorough musical training, which, with his articulate tongue, he can impart to others. Along with this is a personality with charm, scintillating wit, and remarkable vitality.* ❧ *A truly great musician; an intelligent, warm human being; an exciting, inspiring person—he is all of those. I wish him and his family a full, rewarding life.*
MARILYN COSTELLO, *Principal Harp*

Underlying most of my memories of this period are those of the Maestro's uncompromising belief in the deep significance of the art of music to the inner life of us all and the role that a symphony orchestra has to play in enhancing that life, whether it be for an individual or a society. His quick, positive response to a request by the musicians to conduct a Concert for Humanity, *which ultimately coalesced the community and organizations that had been trying for years to limit nuclear weapons,* was a political and artistic statement for which I will always be grateful. He said at that time, "It's my country where they are basing the missiles." ❧ *Those who know me will be surprised to find that I felt one of the most human experiences I have known while rehearsing Haydn's Seven Last Words of Our Saviour on the Cross. His description of the way the music expressed the feelings that a mother must feel having to witness the torture-death of her son caused me to understand, after a thirty-five year career as a professional musician, just how deeply affecting the simplest music can be. One could also understand his antipathy to the concept of concert music as entertainment!* ❧ *One of the great treats in my career came while performing in a small chamber orchestra an all-Mozart concert to raise funds for the homeless — another example of Maestro Muti's view of art serving the community.* ❧ *I can't end these recollections without mentioning his kindness to my stand partner, Ferdinand Maresh, who was dying of cancer. I apologize if the Maestro considers this a violation of privacy, but I know how much it meant to Fred and I'm sure Fred would have liked to have it included.*
NEIL COURTNEY, *Assistant Principal Bass*

TOP: ASSOCIATE PRINCIPAL SECOND VIOLIN ROBERT DE PASQUALE OBSERVES AS RICCARDO MUTI SIGNS AUTOGRAPHS FOR STUDENTS AT HIS MUSIC SCHOOL, 1987.

BOTTOM: ASSOCIATE PRINCIPAL VIOLA JAMES FAWCETT (SECOND FROM RIGHT) AND CONCERTMASTER NORMAN CAROL (R.) CONGRATULATE RICCARDO MUTI ON HIS APPOINTMENT AS MUSIC DIRECTOR, 1979.

Treasured friend of our Academy! For all the cherished memories you have given us, please take with you our heartfelt thanks. And you know that in those memories you will stay within our school, and with its children, always.

ROBERT DE PASQUALE, *Associate Principal Second Violin (and a very grateful Academy of Children's Music)*

Any conductor of international stature should, by definition, possess your understanding of the complex structures of music and your intense allegiance toward projecting the humanity of music through performance. Presently, at least on my wavelength, none, other than you, does.

JAMES FAWCETT, *Associate Principal Viola*

Dear Maestro Muti,

On the day you announced to us that your tenure as Music Director would soon be ending, my first reaction was one of surprise. I did not have the impression that you had completed the task of molding the Orchestra into the perfect musical instrument you wanted us to become. Yet this goal is perhaps one you never would have reached, because for an artist of your calibre, such striving for perfection is a never-ending process. ❧ Next came disappointment. There had been so many unforgettable performances, so many interpretations both exciting and profound. For many of us, the high point was probably the operatic performances. Verdi was, of course, in your blood. But that does not explain how you were able to mesmerize us with Wagner's Flying Dutchman! *❧ Finally, understanding. If you are now at a point in your life where you feel the need for more time, surely no one can begrudge you that. Several years ago I myself enjoyed the benefit of a sabbatical, largely the result of your understanding and support for just such a need. I am sure I speak for all of my colleagues in expressing gratitude to you for the opportunities for personal or professional leave, which are now available to us, and which you wholeheartedly supported. ❧ Thank you, Maestro, for all that you have given us, both individually and collectively.*

AL FILOSA, *Viola*

Dear Maestro,

From my heart, I thank you for the care and sensitivity you have brought to music and the Orchestra! I felt a rapport beyond the ordinary with you; a psychic bond of sorts. I often felt as though I were playing with a fine chamber musician rather than solely following a conductor. Your ability to share the intricacies of the score with a poetic sensibility and your attention to detail made performing interesting and meaningful. Music came alive and I experienced joy in the process. Thank you for enriching my life with your artistry and humanity. I will miss you. ❧ Buon divertimento e con affetto,

JUDY GEIST, *Viola*

We will miss you very much for your musical leadership. Jean joins me in friendship and admiration,
HARRY GORODETZER, *Cello (retired)*

Even though I have been retired since 1983, my memories of playing in the Orchestra under Maestro Muti remain vivid. Please add my congratulations and best wishes.
SAMUEL GORODETZER, *Bass (retired)*

Dear Maestro,
At the announcement of the anniversary of your 20-year association with The Philadelphia Orchestra, I want to share in the tribute and congratulations remembering with nostalgia the many years of wonderful and exciting music-making. My warmest wishes go out to you and your dear family for good health and all your future endeavors.
WOLFGANG GRANAT, *Viola (retired)*

Dear Maestro,
The finest tribute that we could give to you would be to do what you have constantly taught us: To always give our best.
RICHARD HARLOW, *Cello*

Congratulations to Riccardo Muti — conductor, master, and teacher who taught us the correct pronunciation of Alborada, Attila, Zandonai, and told us the meaning of the term Con anima.
MASON JONES, *Principal Horn (retired)*

Thank you, Riccardo, for your marvelous support, from the very beginning, of The Philadelphia Orchestra parties that honor people who are retiring and those who have already retired. This support has been truly appreciated by past and present Orchestra members.
LOUIS LANZA, *Second Violin*

It was the end of a long recording session, the end of a string of recording sessions, and the very end of Tchaikovsky's Francesca da Rimini, where the fires of purgatory were about to engulf Francesca and her lover forever. The gong and the bass drum were roaring, the Orchestra in general was screaming (with the sound whipping around the Memorial Hall basketball gymnasium), when Maestro Muti stopped and said to me, "Break everything." Uh-oh. The intensity of his music-making made it impossible to back away from any requests, whether on stage or in the recording studio. So sure enough, at the height of hell in the final fermata, "rrrrRip" went the calfskin head — humiliation. ❧ Yet, when the CD comes out shortly, one will probably not hear the "rip," but surely will hear intensity, honesty, vitality, integrity — even the fiery desperation of that moment — whose source was from a conductor who never holds back, who is always searching, and we deeply hope will search with us some more along the way.
DON S. LIUZZI, *Principal Timpani*

I got to play with the greatest.
IRVING LUDWIG, *Second Violin (retired)*

RICCARDO AND CRISTINA MUTI WITH THE ORCHESTRA PERCUSSION SECTION, (L. TO R.) ANTHONY ORLANDO, ALAN ABEL, GERALD CARLYSS, MICHAEL BOOKSPAN, AND ANDREW REAMER IN SOUTH AMERICA, 1988.

*The most fruitful and memorable years of my long career with The
Philadelphia Orchestra have been the years spent with Maestro Muti.*

LEONARD MOGILL, *Viola (retired)*

Dear Maestro Muti,

*Words are sometimes so inadequate to express one's feelings. How can we
put into words the many exquisite concerts we had with you or how much
your artistry and dedication have been an inspiration to us! The last
twelve years have been truly wonderful. Moreover, when we think back
on that time, we do not only think of you as a great musician but as a
warm human being, whom we will miss.* ❧ *Thank you for all the wonderful concerts. We wish you and your family much happiness and success.*

DONALD MONTANARO, *Associate Principal Clarinet*

MARGARITA MONTANARO, *Associate Principal Harp*

*Perhaps the most significant part of my relationship with Maestro Muti
has been his support and endorsement of my mission to establish a summer camp for training young musicians, located in Lake Luzerne, N.Y.
Most memorable and meaningful to all was when, during his last visit
to Saratoga Springs, he took time out after five hours of rehearsing to
visit the camp, listen to a student orchestra rehearsal, and then speak to
the students. I am very appreciative of his awareness of the importance
of education in building our future audiences.*

BERT PHILLIPS, *Cello (retired)*

Dear Riccardo,

*To have you as a musical colleague and mentor for so many years would
have been sufficient — but to enjoy your friendship and affection in
addition — that was the ultimate joy!*

IRVIN ROSEN, *Principal Second Violin (retired)*

Salute Maestro Muti!

*I was fortunate enough to have sixteen years with the Maestro. My
forty-two years with the Orchestra were rewarded by those sixteen years.*
❧ *I remember when talking with the Maestro, saying that my one
regret was that I wasn't twenty-five years younger to be able to continue
to make music under him. In his usual gracious manner, he quickly
replied, "You certainly play as if you were twenty-five years younger!"* ❧
*My wife, Judi, and I send our sincere best wishes for your future
achievements and joys.*

SEYMOUR ROSENFELD, *Trumpet (retired)*

Dear Maestro Muti,

*My son, Frank Saam, is a unique example of your dedication to young
students. At an early age Frank expressed the desire to make stringed
instruments. During his elementary school years he apprenticed with a
Philadelphia violin shop, his dream being to one day attend the International School of Violin Making in Cremona, Italy, where Stradivarius and his fellow masters lived and worked.* ❧ *Unfortunately, several
problems occurred, preventing him from entering the school. Upon
hearing of this, you provided advice and assistance, enabling Frank to
appear before the school directors and qualify for enrollment. Now in
his fourth and final year, Frank has produced several violins and a
viola and is presently working on a cello.* ❧ *Without your help, this
dream never would have become reality.*

FRANK E. SAAM, *First Violin*

Dear Maestro Muti,

*The first day you stood before our orchestra I sensed that here was a real
conductor. The ensuing years have proven me correct as you have led us
into consistently high levels of performance. Second best was never good
enough! The operas we did together provided a new dimension to our
musical lives.* ❧ *Viva Verdi! Viva Muti!*

ROGER M. SCOTT, *Principal Bass*

*Maestro Muti is a consummate musician. He has heart, intelligence,
and technique, the three qualities essential to a good musician, in perfect balance.* ❧ *From the first time I heard him conduct in 1973, I was
captivated by the vitality and clarity of the music that came through to
the audience. Later, when I joined the Orchestra, I understood why.
His love and passion for music are so strong that they are infectious,*

but this is always tempered by clear understanding of form and structure, and his ability to communicate these ideas to the musicians, often with humor, is extraordinary. His concept of the music is so convincing that the musicians can feel and express it as if it were their own. His integrity is such that even when the music at hand is a complex contemporary work, he manages to play it in its most accessible light. ❧ Last, but not least, I admire him as a human being. In spite of his well-deserved success, he is kind, sympathetic, and always ready to help others. His selfless dedication to the "Music" and his unwavering loyalty to the musicians inspire us and touch our hearts. Not only a musician of the highest caliber, he is a person of exceptional depth and quality. It has been a privilege to work with him and he will be greatly missed in Philadelphia.

KIYOKO TAKEUTI, *Piano and Celesta*

Throughout the fourteen years that I have played with Riccardo Muti, I never once recall being bored. This is not faint praise. It is the highest praise, for as Pablo Casals once said, "Monotony is the enemy of Music." ❧ If we did a repeat performance of a great but often played classic, he did it with spontaneity, involvement, and love. If he programmed the Salieri Variations on La Follia or a short but exquisite work of Fauré, he found beauty and meaning that would elude a lesser musician. If, by force of circumstance, we did a work that might actually be weak, Muti would never denigrate it but would instead energize

it by his musicality and imagination, so that we, the performers, took up the creative slack left by the composer. ❧ The convergence of intellect, emotion, and integrity that is necessary for an artist to develop these abilities and the courage that must attend their application are rare enough. When this re-creative process is carried out with a sense of humanity, grace, and humor, it is rarer still. ❧ I will always cherish our music-making together and will always admire Riccardo Muti's fidelity to himself and to his muse, and perhaps above all else, his completeness as a human being.

RICHARD WOODHAMS, *Principal Oboe*

Dear Maestro Muti,
When you first began conducting The Philadelphia Orchestra, your expressed interest in urtext editions made the librarians realize that you were seeking precision at a high level. As many of the great romantic orchestra works had not yet been made available in corrected editions, The Philadelphia Orchestra librarians felt that if we could correct the many discrepancies in the printed scores and parts, we would save you and the Orchestra hours of rehearsal time. This work has developed into the most satisfying part of our job, and has allowed our orchestra to become a model for many others who are now using these corrected editions. Thank you for inspiring us to help raise the standards of notation and performance for ourselves, for other orchestras, and for those who follow.

CLINTON F. NIEWEG, *Principal Librarian*

WITH ERIC WOODHAMS, SON OF PRINCIPAL OBOE RICHARD WOODHAMS, 1988

Dear Maestro Muti,

On this very special and, for us, bittersweet occasion, I would like to extend heartfelt gratitude and good wishes to you on behalf of the Board of Directors of The Philadelphia Orchestra Association. ❧ The last two decades, during which you have served as Guest Conductor, Principal Guest Conductor, and Music Director of The Philadelphia Orchestra, have brought new glory to the Orchestra. Your leadership has helped to reaffirm the Orchestra's place as one of the world's greatest musical treasures. ❧ You leave behind a rich legacy, infused with your own uncompromising dedication to the highest standards of artistic excellence. That legacy will serve to remind us of your presence even as you pursue a new chapter of your life. ❧ Let us not say goodbye but arrivederci, for surely we shall meet again when you, as Laureate Conductor, return to this Orchestra to continue the glorious partnership of the last two decades.

JOSEPH NEUBAUER, *Chairman and Chief Executive Officer,*
The Philadelphia Orchestra Association

Riccardo Muti has provided me both enlightenment and inspiration. I have seen him at his calling on stage and off, in rehearsal and concert, preparing and relaxing, touring and recording, greeting well-wishers and patrons, counseling Orchestra members, soloists, and staff alike, studying and instructing, ministering to our present and planning our future. ❧ His uniqueness springs not only from his surpassing musical gifts: it is equally expressed, and even enhanced, by a rare and perfect union of bacchic energy with brilliant apollonian rigor. Each tempered by the other, their whole becomes greater than the sum of their parts.

CATHY BARBASH, *Orchestra Manager*

Dear Maestro Muti,

My introduction to you is one of my most vivid memories. When you shook my hand, you literally lifted my feet off the floor — just as your music has lifted our spirits during the years of your tenure as Music Director. ❧ This is not "goodbye" but rather, "to be continued."

JOY P. BARROWS, *Executive Director, Restoration Fund,*
Academy of Music of Philadelphia, Inc.

Dear Maestro Muti,

How fortunate the Academy of Music has been to have had your music within its walls. You have enhanced our orchestra's international reputation during your tenure, and we are grateful for the years we have enjoyed together. ❧ We wish you well and look forward to your returning often to our stage.

WILLARD S. BOOTHBY, JR.,
President, Academy of Music of Philadelphia, Inc.

Maestro,

It has been a memorable, two-fold association. As marketer, I've known you through checking in before concerts to rescue any unticketed guests and, over the years, speaking with the extensive audience whom you've touched with your music. As photographer, I've spent hours intently watching you through the lens, hoping to have such profound musical moments captured on film. And I warmly remember those times when you would be asked to pose — at a party or backstage — and your eyes would twinkle back at me with a humorous glance.

JEAN E. BRUBAKER,
Director of Marketing and Resident Photographer

I have treasured the year during which I have been associated with The Philadelphia Orchestra, with you as Music Director. It is not nearly long enough, but it is far better than not having had that opportunity at all. I particularly want to express my gratitude for the many occasions on which you took pains to instruct me in the subtleties of public relations for the Orchestra, saying that you wanted me to know these things not only for your tenure but for my future relationship with your successor. ❧ I hope the years ahead will bring you much personal and professional happiness, and that The Philadelphia Orchestra will always be close to your heart. We will miss you greatly.

DIANA BURGWYN, *Director of Public Relations*

Italy, December 1987

Riccardo suggested that Steve and I visit Puglia, the province of his childhood. We walked through seaside towns and marvelled at the stark Norman beauty of the cathedrals, the simplicity and strength of the old masonry walls, the complex patterns of streets and stairways, the intricate evening light as it captured deep openings and bright green doors. Young boys played stick ball among the ancient walls while their grandmamas lovingly washed the cobbled streets, which had been travelled by the armies of Frederick II centuries before. ❧ A week later we were in Milan. We were reminded of the Puglian strength, the light, the clarity,

and the transcendence of time as we listened to the Maestro conduct *Don Giovanni. I had never loved opera more. Through his music Riccardo Muti has shown us the very qualities we discovered on the streets and in the cathedrals and castles of his boyhood.*
GIANNE CONARD *(Mrs. Stephen Sell)*

That we came to know each other
and work together ten years after
we met and liked each other
means to me that there is
a future in which I may still
know you and hear your music
…but first I will miss you.
JUDITH FRANKFURT, *General Manager*

Congratulations on the 20th anniversary of your association with The Philadelphia Orchestra. Like you, I am also enjoying my 20th year with The Philadelphia Orchestra Association. It has always been a pleasure and honor to work with you, especially during these past twelve years as the Music Director. I am looking forward to your return as a guest conductor. ❧ *Like you, this may also be my last season with The Philadelphia Orchestra and the Academy of Music.* ❧ *Congratulations again and best of wishes to you and your lovely wife and family*
GERALD V. KIDDER, *Usher of the Year, 1990, Academy of Music of Philadelphia, Inc. (Mr. Kidder died on January 5, 1992, after a long illness.)*

Dear Maestro,
It is hard to believe that 20 years have elapsed since you first came to Philadelphia and we met. The conversations we have had through the years have been memorable and thought-provoking. And when the subject came to opera, we always had great fun. Some of your stories have been priceless. ❧ *Your years in Philadelphia will always be remembered as great ones. I feel very fortunate to have been able to hear such quantities of beautiful music conducted by you.* ❧ *Thank you for spending so much of your time with us. I wish you and Cristina much health, happiness, and success in the forthcoming years.*
JERRY LENARD, *Usher, Academy of Music of Philadelphia, Inc.*

Dear Maestro Muti,
On behalf of the staff of the Academy of Music, please accept our sincere good wishes for your future. It has been a pleasure to work with you these many years. Your gracious manner with everyone on staff has been deeply appreciated. We will miss your presence backstage as much as our audiences will miss your artistry on stage. Your commitment to educating present and future audiences will enable the Academy of Music seats to be filled for generations to come. Thank you for the legacy you leave

to the history of the Academy of Music. Best regards to you, and your lovely family, for a challenging and fulfilling future. Please come back to your Academy family often; our welcome will always be warm.
ACADEMY OF MUSIC MANAGER'S OFFICE, *Hugh F. Walsh, Jr., John J. Schmidt, Maureen Lynch, and the entire staff and crew of the "Grand Old Lady of Locust Street"*

Dear Maestro Muti,
We first met when your beautiful Cristina and Domenico (newborn) were coming to Philadelphia. A playpen for the baby was the first order of business that fall day in 1979 when Joe Santarlasci commissioned me to accompany you for this purchase. From that day on, my admiration and respect for you and your family have known no bounds, and it has been my great pleasure to have had the opportunity of working with you these many years. Thank you, thank you for your friendship, the time you have given us, and the rewards we have reaped from your presence. Frank and I wish only the best for all of you.
MIMI O'MALLEY, *Secretary to Maestro Muti*

WITH HEAD USHER ANDY PANTANO, 1989

In the 35 years that I have worked for the Academy of Music and The Philadelphia Orchestra, there has never been a more exacting conductor, demanding the best, not only of his musicians but also of the patrons and personnel. His presence here is felt and appreciated. He will be missed but not forgotten. So, as the saying goes, we hate to see you go. And to you and your family I wish you the very best. ❧ *Buona fortuna always,*
ANDY PANTANO, *Head Usher, Academy of Music of Philadelphia, Inc.*

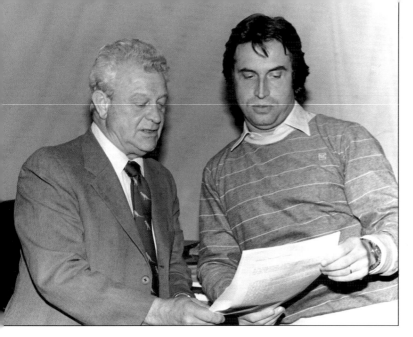

WITH JOSEPH H. SANTARLASCI, SR.

BOYD BARNARD, ORCHESTRA EMERITUS DIRECTOR, CELEBRATES HIS BIRTHDAY AT DINNER WITH THE MUTIS AND FORMER ORCHESTRA CHAIRMAN WILLIAM P. DRAKE AND MRS. DRAKE, DURING THE ORHCESTRA'S 1987 EUROPEAN TOUR.

Dear Riccardo,

How very fortunate The Philadelphia Orchestra has been to have benefitted so greatly from your dynamic personality and superb music-making over the past 20 years. And, I feel most fortunate to have been with the Orchestra during this time and will always cherish the wonderful times and meals we have had together, both in Philadelphia and on tour. ❧ *I know that you have never questioned the deep respect that I have for you, and I hope that Rosemary and I will always be considered friends. We look forward to many more years of your presence here. Salute!*

JOSEPH H. SANTARLASCI, SR., *Assistant Manager (1950–78); Manger (1979–85)*

Dear Maestro,

During the 20 years I have known you, there have been many great performances. I have special memories of your concert performances of opera. I have enjoyed the opportunity to work with you and the good fortune to get to know you. I hope to be able to continue working with you in the future. ❧ *My fondest wishes to you and your family for continued health and happiness. May all your future endeavors be great successes.*

JOHN J. SCHMIDT, *Assistant Manager, Academy of Music of Philadelphia, Inc.*

To know Riccardo Muti is a special privilege. His photographs seldom portray his real likeness, his sense of humor, or the real fun in his character. He can turn every incident and event into humorous conversation. He can be stern with people and situations. He must have respect from his players, but I have heard few rehearsals where there was not frivolity and laughter interspersed with strict discipline. ❧ *I will miss Riccardo; he was a good friend. He has helped me to love music in ways I could not have without him. His love of life and family dictates that he must leave us. But he will be back many times as our guest. We will always love and welcome Riccardo Muti.*

BOYD T. BARNARD, *Emeritus, Board of Directors of The Philadelphia Orchestra Association*

My Dear Maestro,

As Music Director of The Philadelphia Orchestra you have enhanced the vibrancy of the musical life in our community, and for this we are immensely grateful. On a more personal note, I have enjoyed our encounters and look forward to more in the future, keeping in mind your words to me when I responded that I was nervous before playing a movement of a Beethoven quartet in front of an audience which included yourself —"La forza del destino!"

PETER A. BENOLIEL, *Vice President (1982–91), Board of Directors of The Philadelphia Orchestra Association*

Your Bach B-minor Mass was truly superb and remains one of my treasured memories of the Maestro and the Orchestra.

MRS. T. WISTAR BROWN, *Assistant Secretary (1984–87); Secretary (1987–89), Board of Directors of The Philadelphia Orchestra Association*

Dear Riccardo,

Although I share with your many friends here a sense of loss as you loosen your ties to The Philadelphia Orchestra, a much stronger feeling is that of gratitude for your twenty years of personal dedication and artistic leadership. Under your tutelage, the Orchestra has grown in all the important dimensions so that it is now acknowledged as being unsurpassed anywhere. ❧ *I feel especially privileged, particu-*

larly in the last three years, in having been able to share a few informal moments with you, and I am enormously grateful for your unswerving and articulate support of our efforts to provide the Orchestra with the concert hall it deserves. ❧ There is no greater luxury than having time to think, to write, to relax, and to enjoy your family. Please take the fullest advantage of it.

CRISTINA MUTI WITH DAVID AND SANDY EASTBURN, 1988

THEODORE A. BURTIS, *Vice President (1987–88); President (1988–91), Board of Directors of The Philadelphia Orchestra Association*

My dear Maestro,

Twenty years can speed by quickly! It is hard to realize that your association with The Philadelphia Orchestra dates back to 1972, but it is easy to recognize your wonderful contributions, particularly over the past 12 years you have served as Music Director. ❧ Your energy, integrity, creativeness, and scholarship have enriched our orchestra and thrilled and stimulated audiences in Philadelphia and throughout the world. ❧ On a more personal note, Peggy and I have greatly enjoyed knowing Cristina and you and sharing some memorable and happy moments, such as the 1986 opening night at Teatro alla Scala, your anniversary party in Saõ Paulo during the South American tour in 1988, and the concert at the Musikverein during last year's European tour. ❧ We thank you warmly for your significant contributions to Philadelphia's cultural and intellectual life and look forward to your continuing association with The Philadelphia Orchestra.

M. TODD COOKE, *President (1986–88); Chairman (1988–91), Board of Directors of The Philadelphia Orchestra Association*

Dear Riccardo,

I have thought of you often since I retired as Chairman of the Board of the Orchestra. We are all grateful for all you have done for The Philadelphia Orchestra. One of my pleasures was to see how you matured as a person while Music Director of our orchestra, and I feel privileged to have developed a friendship that I shall cherish over the rest of my life. Margie and I will particularly remember our trips with you and Cristina to Europe and the Far East. ❧ I know there are things we have both left undone, but a great deal has been achieved, and I am delighted that in years to come we shall still see you from time to time. Margie joins me in thanks and affectionate good will.

WILLIAM P. DRAKE, *Emeritus, Vice President and Chairman (1978–88), Board of Directors of The Philadelphia Orchestra Association*

Dear Riccardo,

When I press the rewind button, a lot of familiar pictures flash on the screen. The thrill of standing on the podium at rehearsal to inform the Orchestra that the Board had selected you as their leader. Talking in my living room about how to squeeze one more week out of your schedule. Triumphs on tour. Trips to the Amish country. And, of course, the music. For some, music may soothe the savagery in their breasts, but for us — at least when it's Muti and The Philadelphia Orchestra — the response is unalloyed excitement. ❧ But throughout all this, faces keep flashing on the screen. The men and women who have blown their lungs out, suffered pinched nerves, traveled direct from Italy to the stage in London, recorded on weekends, poured out their problems to you, sighed in relief when you boarded the plane for Italy only to count the days until you came back. ❧ I think I've got it after all: you, Cristina, Sandy and I all care about the same people.

DAVID P. EASTBURN, *President (1978–85); Chairman (1985–86), Board of Directors of The Philadelphia Orchestra Association*

Most of us have received many honors during our careers, but few have had the honor that I was awarded by the kiss that was bestowed on me by Cristina Muti, the beautiful wife of the new Music Director. She graced the receiving line at the reception that I, as President of the Academy of Music, hosted before the Annual Concert and Ball. ❧

CRISTINA MUTI WITH J. LIDDON PENNOCK, JR.

Early in the 1980s, Riccardo and Cristina Muti accepted my invitation to see the Philadelphia Flower Show. After they admired the exhibits, I felt that they might enjoy the famous Awards Luncheon held in the ballroom. I had explained that the instant we finished lunch we should make a fast exit before the endless awards ceremonies began. After dessert I gave Riccardo the "let's get out of here" signal which he, seated next to the president of the Horticultural Society, totally ignored. Finally, I had to stand up and repeat it. The effect on Riccardo was simply to induce him to also stand. Despite his unfamiliarity with the English language, he hissed at me "rude, rude Leedon." He then sat down and remained throughout the entire ceremony.

J. LIDDON PENNOCK, JR., *Emeritus Director, Vice President (1974–80); President (1980–88), Academy of Music of Philadelphia, Inc.*

VOLUNTEER COMMITTEES

AN AUTOGRAPH PARTY 1988

Dear Maestro Muti,

The 600 members of the Orchestra's Volunteer Committees join me in expressing appreciation and gratitude to you for your unstinting dedication and cooperation over the years in our efforts and activities on behalf of the Orchestra. Your willing participation in press conferences, donor recognition events, autograph parties, Opening Night, Radiothon, and other such occasions added a special dimension which not only assured the success of the event but added a special glow to the festivities. ❧ Your many friends and admirers among the Volunteers, and indeed the entire Orchestra family, hope and trust that you will return to Philadelphia regularly and frequently in the ensuing years, and that we can look forward again to being mesmerized, not only by your genius as a conductor, but by your charm, wit, and gracious personality. ❧ We recognize that your illustrious career has attained unparalleled heights in the United States and indeed the entire world — and as you continue ever forward we wish you and all of your family good health and happiness in the days ahead. ❧ With warmest affection,

WITH VOLUNTEER COMMITTEES
PRESIDENT DORIS FRANKEL

DORIS G. FRANKEL, *President, Volunteer Committees for The Philadelphia Orchestra*

Bravissimo! You have enriched our lives with your remarkable concerts, from the classical to the contemporary, during a score of years. Your welcome to the youthful students at the rehearsals will inspire the future audiences for The Philadelphia Orchestra. You have a special niche in our lives — Arrivederci.

MRS. ELIZABETH SCHOCH BOWDEN, *Chairman of the Rittenhouse Square Committee for The Philadelphia Orchestra*

Riccardo,

Your commitment to the highest standards of interpretation have given me a much deeper appreciation and understanding of great music. You have been open and generous with your time and your talents. In addition, you have reached out to the community to teach and encourage our young. You have become a member of our community. Thank you for all you have done. I will miss you. May you continue to enjoy great success and fulfillment in your life.

LAURA (MRS. ORVILLE H). BULLITT, JR., *Vice-Chairman, Muti Tribute Gala Committee*

Dear Maestro,

As you end your tenure with The Philadelphia Orchestra, I would like to express my great admiration for your superb musicianship and my gratitude for your support during my presidency of the Volunteer Committees for The Philadelphia Orchestra. In particular, your great interest in the musical education of young people has been special to me, as was your generous participation in planning the first Opening Night Gala. ❧ The April 22 tribute to you, which I have had the honor of chairing, is a small, though hopefully appropriate way in which we can express our deep appreciation and our warmest wishes as you approach the next stage in your illustrious career.

MRS. DAVID L. PENNINGTON, *Chairman, Muti Tribute Gala Committee; Immediate Past President, The Volunteer Committees for The Philadelphia Orchestra*

In March of 1978, I had the privilege of singing (as a member of the Choral Arts Society) under the baton of Maestro Muti for the first time. This occasion inspired me so deeply that I decided at that time to become an active volunteer for The Philadelphia Orchestra as soon as I would retire from my teaching position. Since then, the Maestro has provided me with many additional musical experiences, including attendance at regular and special concerts, and recordings with the Orchestra. I now include these among my most memorable highlights, and I have also found that my work with the Volunteer Committees has become ever increasingly enjoyable. ❧ I give my thanks to you, Maestro, for all that you have given me and Philadelphia with your professional leadership, and extend my best wishes for your continued leadership in the world of music.

MRS. JOHN W. EDGAR, *Rittenhouse Square Committee for The Philadelphia Orchestra*

OPENING NIGHT COMMITTEE, 1989: (L. TO R. FRONT ROW) JANET KLAUS, MAISIE HOLLENBACH, POLLY NEWBOLD, ELIZABETH BOWDEN, BARBARA TAYLOR (L. TO R. BACK ROW) MARTHA KENNEDY, ALEX PENNINGTON, HELEN JUSTI, CAROL BARKER, CRISTINA MUTI, LAURA BULLITT, ELIA BUCK, BETH GLENDINNING

Dear Maestro Muti,

Thanks for the beautiful memories.

ISABEL KELLER, *Central Committee for The Philadelphia Orchestra*

Dear Riccardo,

As I look back on twenty years of friendship with you, I am reminded of many meaningful times. You were a very special guest at the post-concert dinner parties that Philip and I held, as was Cristina, whose beauty and charm captivated us. ❧ Some of my most vivid memories relate to your association with the Art Alliance, a unique Philadelphia institution that honored you with its Medal of Achievement in recognition of your commitment to the musical education of young people. I also remember the 75th anniversary of the Art Alliance, at which you were guest of honor, just as Leopold Stokowski, a founder of the Alliance, had been on its 50th anniversary. ❧ I hope we will share many such wonderful times together in the future.

ESTHER KLEIN, *President Emeritus, Rittenhouse Square Committee for The Philadelphia Orchestra*

WITH ESTHER KLEIN, DURING THE 1991 EUROPEAN TOUR

Maestro, I treasure the memory of explaining to you the role of "la volontaria." You were a quick study!

POLLY NEWBOLD, *Past President (1982–85), The Volunteer Committees for The Philadelphia Orchestra*

Dear Maestro Muti,

I am extremely grateful to you for literally educating my ears during your tenure as Music Director. My appreciation for contemporary music has increased as I now find beauty and inspiration in new works that formerly fell on deaf ears. The concert operas that you have programmed yearly have given me an awareness and appreciation of opera and its composers not previously held. ❧ And I totally believe and am an enthusiastic supporter of your credo: that "music enriches the soul." ❧ I feel very honored and privileged to have had the opportunity to know you and your wife, and hope to maintain some contact in the future.

SUSIE (MRS. NORMAN P.) ROBINSON, *Vice President, The Volunteer Committees for The Philadelphia Orchestra and member of the Board of Directors of The Philadelphia Orchestra Association*

Dear Maestro Muti,

The celebration of your twenty years in Philadelphia is a poignant one for all of us who hold you in such high regard. ❧ Bill and I have lived in Philadelphia for nearly ten years, and during that time you have affect-

MAESTRO MUTI CONFERS WITH (L. TO R.) SALLY HARRAL, LAURA BULLITT, AND ALEXANDRA PENNINGTON, AS THEY PREPARE FOR THE 1990 OPENING NIGHT PRESS PARTY.

ed our lives much more than you could ever be aware. We have observed you working tirelessly throughout the days and nights, lifting The Philadelphia Orchestra's music to the highest standard of perfection. We so admire you and our musicians that I fear we never rushed to your side to thank you as we should have. Instead, we gave you privacy and rest from the hectic schedule you endure. I wonder if our actions caused you to feel friendless in this city, but fervently hope that that is not so. ❧ We rejoice knowing that as Laureate Conductor you will be returning often to conduct the Orchestra. We assure you that the dream of a new concert hall will not be laid to rest! Our orchestra and our city desperately need such a cultural center if we are to remain vital on the world's stage. ❧ We thank both you and Mrs. Muti for giving all of us twenty beautiful years of your lives. Paraphrasing a quotation written by Winston Churchill to Franklin D. Roosevelt, Bill and I feel so very fortunate to have shared this decade with you! ❧ With warmest admiration,

BARBARA (MRS. WILSON H.) TAYLOR, *Central Committee for The Philadelphia Orchestra; Co-Chairman, Academy of Music 135th Anniversary Concert and Ball*

Maestro Muti, your introduction of new works into the regular orchestra repertoire has helped educate Philadelphia in the sound of classical music today, and Philadelphia and its citizens are richer because of these gifts. ❧ Maestro Muti, you have touched the hearts and ears of Philadelphians and people throughout the world, and all we can offer you is our eternal thanks and our best wishes. ❧ With sincere appreciation,

PEGGY WEBER, *Chestnut Hill Committee for The Philadelphia Orchestra*

Dear Maestro Muti,
We are justifiably proud of "our" Orchestra, and in the past had been of the opinion that improvement was not necessary and probably not possible. ❧ You challenged that opinion and challenged the Orchestra. We watched and listened as, under your guidance and inspiration, the Orchestra grew in versatility and in richness of expression. You have taught us an unforgettable lesson: that greatness is not good enough, that there is always a need and ample room to grow. ❧ We thank you for that and wish for you continued challenge and growth.

BETTY-SCHUYLER D. WOOD, *Chairman, Opening Night 1992*

FRIENDS AND COLLEGUES

Dear Maestro Muti,
As you leave Philadelphia, you take with you the deepest gratitude of all Philadelphians for your leadership in the preservation and continuance of the grand tradition of our beloved Philadelphia Orchestra. ❧ My prayers and best wishes go with you as you continue to share your musical gifts with all music lovers everywhere.

ANTHONY CARDINAL BEVILACQUA VISITS BACKSTAGE AFTER A CONCERT, 1988.

ANTHONY CARDINAL BEVILACQUA, *Archbishop of Philadelphia*

Dear Maestro Muti,
For more than 25 years, Fidelity Bank has had the pleasure of supporting Philadelphia's world-class orchestra. On behalf of our employees and customers, I would like to thank you for continuing and expanding that long tradition of excellence. ❧ Philadelphia has been privileged to have an artist of your caliber leading one of our most treasured institutions. And we have been even more fortunate that your artistry has not been limited to our city, but has been displayed all over the world. You have been an international ambassador for our city, and the reflection of your presence has made Philadelphia shine brighter everywhere. ❧ We wish you continued success.

ROLAND K. BULLARD II, *President and Chief Executive Officer, Fidelity Bank*

Dear Riccardo,
It seems like only yesterday, but sixteen years have passed since I first came to Philadelphia to meet you and attend your concert. My! Was I impressed with this young man who conducted with the intensity of

Toscanini and looked like a matinée idol. I could never express in words what our relationship has meant to me all these years. The memories of all the sublime performances, the myriad of great recordings that I was privileged to be a part of, the lunches and dinners and the awful breakfasts at the recording hall where we shared our love for music and exchanged ideas and thoughts, plus your wonderful sense of humor that would send me off into gales of laughter. These are memories that will be part of me forever. ❧ You have enlightened and taught me more about music than I could ever have imagined. You are the true maestro, the consummate musician and teacher. Yet with all your prodigious talent and abilities, the thing that has most impressed me is your loyalty and friendship. That is something I will always cherish.

TONY CARONIA, *Vice President, Artist Relations, Angel/EMI Records*

Riccardo Muti is a symphony of style. It is the good fortune of many Philadelphians to have shared the same lifetime with him. He is the best man with a stick in his hand since Mike Schmidt. We do not plan to miss him—we plan to remember him.

RICHARD P. JACKMAN, *Director of Communications, Sun Company, Inc.*

Dear Riccardo,
In each lifetime, some of us are privileged to experience magical moments — moments of great beauty, of great depth, of great caring, and of great devotion. Such are the moments when you share your gift of making music, and for these special occasions we continue to be full of gratitude. In short, you are the best! ❧ As friends, Nick and I remain devoted and wish for you and your family continued happiness and good health. He joins me in sending love and admiration.

MARY LOU FALCONE, *M.L. Falcone Public Relations*

Dear Riccardo,
All the concerts in Philadelphia and on tour in Vienna, Salzburg, and in La Scala have been glorious. What stand out most for me are your electric music-making, your blazing integrity, and the post-concert anecdotes, which often have left me speechless. Without you I would

PRESENTING A PLAQUE OF APPRECIATION TO ANGEL/EMI VICE PRESIDENT TONY CARONIA, ON BEHALF OF THE PHILADELPHIA ORCHESTRA ASSOCIATION, 1988

never have really known what little I have learned about Italy or the Italian language. I look forward to as many lifetimes as we can squeeze in of working together.

DAVID V. FOSTER, *Vice President, Columbia Artists Management, Inc.*

Our lives have been enriched with unforgettable musical experiences and lasting inspiration…You are leaving us but we will hold Muti the maestro, Muti the man, and his beautiful family close to our hearts forever.

ENZO AND CARLA FUSARO, *Ristorante Il Gallo Nero*

Dear Maestro Muti,
As co-sponsor of the Gala and Tribute Concert in your honor, LEXUS is extremely proud of its affiliation with The Philadelphia Orchestra. ❧ We are especially pleased and honored to have been associated with the Orchestra during the last three seasons of your term as Music Director. Under your masterful direction, the Orchestra's performances have been a rare pleasure and have made a lasting impact in Philadelphia and throughout the world over the past twenty years. ❧ Please accept our congratulations and best wishes for continued success. We look forward to seeing you again many times in Philadelphia in your new role as Laureate Conductor.

J. DAVIS ILLINGWORTH, JR., *Group Vice President and General Manager, LEXUS*

Frolic Weymouth, Pete, and I remember with pleasure our times with you — both at The Philadelphia Orchestra and when you came with us on a carriage ride to a beautiful pastoral hill for a picnic. There you expressed your desire to conduct the Orchestra in Beethoven's 6th. We will miss you.

ELISE & PETE duPONT AND FROLIC WEYMOUTH

ORIGINAL WATERCOLOR OF HORSEDRAWN CARRIAGE BY FROLIC WEYMOUTH

Dear Maestro,

The Philadelphia Orchestra has had a long history of firsts in the USA: the first Orchestra to perform on its own national radio broadcast, the first on national TV, and the first Orchestra to make recordings with its own conductor. Philips Classics Productions is proud to have added another first to this illustrious list: the first recording we made with you was with The Philadelphia Orchestra. ❧ Our four-year relationship cannot compete with two decades, but the enthusiasm and dedication we feel is reflected in wonderful recordings we have made with you and The Philadelphia Orchestra. ❧ Thank you for the past and look forward to a long future.

HANS KINZL, *President, Philips Classics Productions*

WITH DR. HANS KINZL, PRESIDENT OF PHILIPS CLASSICS, 1988

Dear Riccardo,

Every moment we have spent with you has been a joyful and memorable experience. You are not only endowed with a brilliant mind and extraordinary ability to maintain rapport with your friends, but every time we saw you conducting we felt the transmission of your enthusiasm and feeling for the extraordinary music you performed in Philadelphia. ❧ We will miss you greatly, and it will be difficult to look at the podium at the Academy without Muti. The only consolation for us is to know that you will have a little more time to enjoy life. ❧ This is not a goodbye but au revoir.

HILARY AND IRENA KOPROWSKI

I couldn't remember being more nervous about a dinner. Not only was I meeting the Music Director of The Philadelphia Orchestra, but I knew that if I was going to get its public relations director to marry me, his approval would go a long way. After dinner, when we listened to the last act of La forza del destino, I speechlessly watched as he conducted, translated, and explained everything for my benefit. In spite of my lack of musical sophistication, he never made me feel foolish or ignorant. In the many times he has taught me since then, it has always been the same. He has always made me feel that the respect was mutual (his father is a physician). He is one of the most decent people I have ever known and one of the best friends I've ever had.

DR. WARREN KURNICK

My dear Maestro Muti,

In summoning the highest virtuosity from the members of The Philadelphia Orchestra for more than a decade, your leadership has been an inspiration to men and women in all walks of life who would call forth the best in those with whom they work. ❧ Not for that reason alone, your farewell this spring to the Orchestra and our country will be bittersweet indeed — especially for those of us present at the Academy of Music in 1972 on the joyous occasion of your United States debut. For twenty years since that evening, your performances have stirred and delighted American audiences, who will soon have the thrill of anticipating your return from time to time. ❧ Especially on behalf of the people of SmithKline Beecham, then, permit me to borrow from Sir Thomas Beecham in expressing our wish that you will be able to return here often as an honored guest. It is reported, as you may know, that Sir Thomas once ventured to a musician at rehearsal, "We cannot expect you to be with us all the time, but perhaps you could be good enough to keep in touch now and again."

THOMAS M. LANDIN, *Chairman, SmithKline Beecham Foundation*

Maestro,

We have been thrilled by your performances and enchanted by you personally over the years. Thank you for two decades of excellence!

TERRENCE A. LARSEN, *Chairman, CoreStates Financial Corp.*

Carissimo Riccardo,

How can we commit to paper the summation of more than twenty years of magnificent music and warm friendship? At a loss for those perfect words, we searched the tomes of literature, both Italian and English, in hopes of borrowing a phrase or two to eloquently express our feelings of gratitude for your friendship, for your music, and for the generosity of spirit with which you both shared often at great personal sacrifice. In the midst of life's daily problems, both global and personal, you created beauty and let us enter into its enchanted world. ❧ Alas, our vocabulary is not as rich as yours. No glorious Beethoven's Ninth, no sublime Mozart's Jupiter, no passionate Tchaikovsky's Fifth, no dramatic Nabucco, no unforgettable Don Giovanni will spring from our pen. Only those two most humble, inadequate words…thank you! You have enriched our lives with your friendship, and our souls with your music.

SERGIO AND PENNY PROSERPI

Sono passati tanti anni del tempo in cui ho conosciuto il Maestro Muti, ed é nata in noi una grande simpatìa, che poi è diventata una grande amicizia. Io ringrazio il Maestro Muti di avermi suggerito l'amore per la musica classica più di quanto l'amavo prima, grazie a lui come artista. Nei confronti dell'amico, non posso trovare parole per potermi esprimere. Ogni volta che farò qualche pettinatura a qualche signora, preparandola per andare al concerto, mi ricorderò di te, Maestro, che passavi di corsa e faticato, ma sempre con un grande saluto, e un sorriso. ✣ Il tuo amico,

DINO TAORMINA

Many years have passed by since I met Maestro Muti and in that time a mutual good understanding has grown into a strong friendship. I thank Maestro Muti the artist for having prompted in me a greater love for classical music than I felt before. As for the friendship, it is difficult to express the feelings in words. In the years to come, every time I am preparing the hair for a lady who will be going to the concert, I will remember you, Maestro, who passed by my shop in a hurry and often tired, but always with a big greeting and a smile. ✣ *Your friend,*
DINO TAORMINA

With appreciation to Riccardo Muti:
For his special contribution of the concert opera — Muti-style — to the Philadelphia stage. One of my most memorable personal musical experiences of a lifetime was attendance at Maestro Muti's truly inspired performance of the Verdi Requiem in honor of the late Eugene Ormandy. Grand Opera took on a new dimension here under the Muti baton.
RICHARD C. TORBERT, *Vice President for Corporate Affairs,* Mellon Bank, N.A.

Maestro Muti,
The glory of your music has brightened the lives of millions of people around the world. As a proud supporter of The Philadelphia Orchestra, we have been honored by your presence, enraptured by your brilliance, and enriched by your dedication. May your future be filled with the sounds and sights of a world made better by your contribution.
ROBERT M. VALENTINI, *President & Chief Executive Officer,* Bell of Pennsylvania

Denise and I relished Riccardo's and Cristina's ironic wit. One of our favorite quotations of his, as a response to our mutual expression of frustration as managers as well as artists in the late 20th century — he as a music director of a symphony orchestra, we as proprietors of a professional office, was: "The only time I get to relax is when I conduct."
ROBERT VENTURI, *Venturi, Scott Brown & Associates, Inc.*

Dear Riccardo,
It has been a real privilege for Judy, Jenny, and me to know you and Cristina and to count you among our friends. While these messages appropriately will include many accolades about your achievements in music, what impresses me most about you is your great depth of knowledge about so many other things, as well. You are, indeed, the true Renaissance man. ✣ I do sincerely hope you will take time not only to smell the roses, but also to count their petals.
EDWARD D. VINER, M.D. *Philadelphia Orchestra Tour Physician*

A Message on behalf of Riccardo Muti's Friends in Europe:
In a nation primarily devoted to the pursuit of material wealth, culture is a necessary condition of the preservation of human values. And of all forms of culture, as we have been told through the ages by such thinkers as Plato and Goethe, music is the highest, the most expressive of what lies in the soul of man. ✣ It should surprise no one, therefore, that in that most vital of nations, the United States of America, there should exist some of the finest orchestras of the world, and that traditionally they should have vied with each other to attract the best from the European scene for their music directors. ✣ Marriages between old orchestras and new music directors have not always been successful, but The Philadelphia Orchestra has found true fulfillment in its association with Riccardo Muti. The Orchestra has loved him for twenty years, and he them, with exemplary devotion and loyalty. What is the result? A brilliant ensemble renowned the world over, and the best musically America can offer. ✣ Players and singers respond to Muti as to no other conductor; they find under his direction qualities they didn't know were in them. With tenderness, humor, and, above all, the most profound understanding of the musical subject involved, he charms from them optimum performances whilst at the same time giving them and his audiences new insights into the music and its interpretation. ✣ Having taken in European classicism with the air he breathed from his childhood days in Naples onwards, amplified and refined by a thorough musical and philosophical education, he has brought to the New World the best culturally of the Old. ✣ Philadelphia has been lucky to have him, and his bonds with the Orchestra will not be eternally severed in 1992. But we never meant him to spend so much of the last twenty years with you, and now Europe needs him back.

LORD WEINSTOCK, *London*

MAESTRO MUTI STANDS ON THE SITE OF THE PROPOSED ORCHESTRA HALL WITH (L. TO R.) SONDRA MYERS, CULTURAL ADVISOR TO THE GOVERNOR OF PENNSYLVANIA, AND DENISE SCOTT BROWN AND ROBERT VENTURI OF THE PHILADELPHIA FIRM VENTURI, SCOTT BROWN, ARCHITECTS FOR THE NEW HALL, 1989.

CLOSING LETTERS

ONE OF THE FIRST MEETINGS BETWEEN
THE MUTIS AND THE ORMANDYS, IN
FLORENCE, 1970

MRS. EUGENE ORMANDY VISITS WITH
THE MUTIS BACKSTAGE, 1992.

MRS. EUGENE ORMANDY
THE BARCLAY
RITTENHOUSE SQUARE
PHILADELPHIA, PENNSYLVANIA 19103

December 9, 1991

Dear Riccardo:

This is where it all began. We had great expectations but never could have imagined it would be so wonderful. I am sad that your time in Philadelphia was so short. But we also knew from the beginning that the world would be beckoning.

However, this is not goodbye. You will be coming back and I possibly might see you wherever you will be.

Affectionately,

Gretel

Gretel Ormandy

Dear and Admired Maestro Muti:

With these few words I wish to express both my gratitude and congratulations. More than ten years ago, you undertook a formidable task in Philadelphia. Looking back now, it certainly led to a very special achievement during a significant period of your professional life. How grandly you succeeded — not only in continuing, but also in furthering the unique tradition of The Philadelphia Orchestra, for which not only I as your colleague, but also many others most sincerely thank you. Now, as you turn your attention and devote yourself to other undertakings, you will be glad of the memories of your American years. ❧ As your successor, I will soon have the opportunity to conduct this wonderful Orchestra, a privilege which I will certainly treasure. My sincere good wishes accompany you throughout all your future plans and endeavors. ❧ In the hope that we shall soon meet again, and with very best wishes, I remain yours

WOLFGANG SAWALLISCH, *Music Director–Designate*

WOLFGANG SAWALLISCH, MUSIC DIRECTOR-
DESIGNATE OF THE PHILADELPHIA ORCHESTRA,
VISITS BACKSTAGE DURING THE ORCHESTRA'S
1991 EUROPEAN TOUR.

BAYERISCHE STAATSOPER
Der Staatsoperndirektor

8000 München 1
Brieffach
Telefon (089) 2 18 51

Ill. mo. Maestro
Riccardo Muti
THE PHILADELPHIA ORCHESTRA

Dezember 1991

Verehrter und lieber Maestro Muti,

meine Zeilen sollen Dank und Glückwunsch zugleich sein. Vor über 10 Jahren haben Sie eine Aufgabe in Philadelphia übernommen, die - jetzt rückblickend - ganz sicher zu einem besonderen Leistungs - und Lebensabschnitt in Ihrer beruflichen Tätigkeit geworden ist. Wie großartig es Ihnen gelungen ist, die einzigartige Tradition des Philadelphia Orchesters weiterzuführen und weiter zu entwickeln, dafür drücke nicht nur ich als Kollege Ihnen einen herzlichen Dank aus. Wenn Sie sich nun entschlossen haben, sich neuen Aufgaben zuzuwenden, werden Sie die amerikanischen Jahre in Ihrer Erinnerung nicht missen wollen.

Die Möglichkeit, nun als ihr Nachfolger dieses wunderbare Orchester leiten zu dürfen, weiß ich sehr wohl zu schätzen.

Mein aufrichtiger Glückwunsch soll Sie bei allen Ihren zukünftigen Plänen und Aufgaben begleiten.

In der Hoffnung auf eine baldige persönliche Wiederbegegnung und den besten Grüßen bin ich Ihr

APPENDIX

❦

BROADCASTS

1980

Verdi: The Requiem Mass, filmed at the Cathedral Basilica of Sts. Peter and Paul, Philadelphia; Katia Ricciarelli, Florence Quivar, Veriano Luchetti, Simon Estes, Mendelssohn Club

1981

The Fabulous Philadelphians: From Ormandy to Muti, a six-part television series co-produced with WHYY-TV, airs nationwide on PBS.

Concert from NHK Hall, Tokyo: Tchaikovsky, Symphony No. 6, *Pathétique*; Mussorgsky-Ravel, *Pictures at an Exhibition*

1982–89

CIGNA/Philadelphia Orchestra Radio Network, broadcasting Orchestra concerts nationwide during 39-week season to more than 300 radio stations throughout the U.S. Several concerts broadcast in Europe and Asia

1985

Symphonie fantastique: A Conductor's View airs nationally on PBS.

It's Your Orchestra Week concert: free concert in Academy of Music broadcast live on WIOQ-FM as part of week-long outreach to new audiences

Concert taped at Bunka Kaikan, Tokyo, Japan: Fine, Notturno for Strings and Harp; Stravinsky, Suite from *L'Oiseau de feu*; Mahler, Symphony No. 1

1987

Concert taped at Alte Oper, Frankfurt, Germany, for West German TV: Verdi, Overture to *La forza del destino*; Stravinsky, Suite from *L'Oiseau de feu* (1919 version); Strauss, *Aus Italien,* Symphonic Fantasy; Martucci, *Notturno* (encore)

1988

Concert taped at Teatro Colón, Buenos Aires, Argentina, for Argentine TV: Beethoven, *Leonore* Overture No. 3, Symphony No. 4, and Symphony No. 5; Verdi, Overture to *La forza del destino*; Martucci, *Notturno* (encores)

1989

Concert taped at Suntory Hall, Tokyo, Japan, for Japanese television and radio: Beethoven, Symphony No. 3, *Eroica;* Ravel, *Rapsodie espagnole* and *Boléro;* Verdi, Overture to *I vespri siciliani* (encore).

Come and Meet the Music: Muti gives spoken introductions to program. Beethoven, Symphony No. 4; Stravinsky, *Orpheus,* Ballet in Three Scenes; Ravel, *Boléro*. Broadcast live on KYW-TV and WFLN-FM.

Brahms, *Haydn* Variations; Schumann, Cello Concerto (with Yo-Yo Ma, cello); Brahms, Symphony No. 1. Broadcast live on KYW-TV and Arts & Entertainment Network, simulcast on WHYY-FM.

1990

Come and Meet the Music: Muti gives spoken introductions to program. Rossini, Overture to *Il barbiere di Siviglia*; Stravinsky, Divertimento: Suite from the Ballet *Le Baiser de la fée*; Beethoven, Symphony No. 3, *Eroica*. Broadcast live on KYW-TV and Arts & Entertainment Network, simulcast on WHYY-FM.

1991

Muti gives spoken introductions to program. Petrassi, *Coro di morti*; Mozart, Requiem: Arleen Auger, Susanne Mentzer, Jozef Kundlak, Simon Estes, Westminster Symphonic Choir. Broadcast live on KYW-TV, simulcast on WHYY-FM.

.Come and Meet the Music: Tribute to Dr. Martin Luther King, Jr.: concert on theme of freedom, with former '76'ers basketball star Julius Erving as narrator for Copland's *Lincoln Portrait*. Broadcast live on KYW-TV and Arts & Entertainment Network, simulcast on WHYY-FM.

Gala Tribute Concert to Riccardo Muti: Carol Vaness, Frederica von Stade, Luciano Pavarotti, Samuel Ramey, Kyung-Wha Chung, Gidon Kremer; Westminster Symphonic Choir. Broadcast live on KYW-TV and Arts & Entertainment Network, simulcast on WFLN-FM.

RICCARDO MUTI DISCOGRAPHY

BACH

Brandenburg Concerto No. 2: Philharmonia Orchestra with Maurice André, trumpet (1984) EMI 7 49474 2

BALAKIREV

Islamey: Philharmonia Orchestra with Andrei Gavrilov, piano EMI 7 69125 2

BARTÓK

Piano Concerto No. 2: RAI Symphony Orchestra of Milan with Dino Ciani, piano (1969) CETRA 1055

BEETHOVEN

Symphony No. 1: Philadelphia Orchestra (1985) EMI 7 49488 2

Symphony No. 2: Philadelphia Orchestra (1987) EMI 7 49488 2

Symphony No. 3, *Eroica*: Philadelphia Orchestra (1987) EMI 7 49490 2

Symphony No. 4: Philadelphia Orchestra (1985) EMI 7 49489 2

Symphony No. 5: Philadelphia Orchestra (1985) EMI 7 49488 2

Symphony No. 6, *Pastorale*: Philadelphia Orchestra (1987) EMI 7 49491 2

Symphony No. 6, *Pastorale*: Philadelphia Orchestra (1978) LP EMI 069 03501

Symphony No. 7: Philadelphia Orchestra (1988) EMI 7 49492 2

Symphony No. 7: Philadelphia Orchestra (1978) LP EMI 069 03472

Symphony No. 8: Philadelphia Orchestra (1987) EMI 7 49492 2

Symphony No. 9, *Choral*: Philadelphia Orchestra with Studer, Ziegler, Seiffert, Morris; Westminster Symphonic Choir (1988) EMI 7 49490 2

Overture, *Consecration of the House*: Philadelphia Orchestra (1985) EMI 7 49490 2

Overture to *Fidelio*: Philadelphia Orchestra (1985) EMI 49490 2

Leonore Overture No. 3: Philadelphia Orchestra (1988) EMI 49491 2

The Beethoven Nine Symphonies and three overtures are also published as a set: EMI 7 49487 2

Piano Concerto No. 3: Philharmonia Orchestra with Sviatoslav Richter, piano (1977) EMI 69013 2

Piano Concerto No. 4: Philadelphia Orchestra with Claudio Arrau, piano

BELLINI

I Puritani with Caballé, Kraus, Manuguerra, Hamari, Ferrin; Ambrosian Opera Chorus and Philharmonia Orchestra (1979) EMI 7 69633 2

I Capuleti e i Montecchi with Gruberova, Baltsa, Raffanti, Howell, Tomlinson; Chorus and Orchestra of Covent Garden (1984) EMI 78 47388 2

I Capuleti e i Montecchi with Freni, Pavarotti, Bruscantini, Fiorentini, Giaiotti; RAI Chorus and Orchestra of Rome (1969) Nuova Era 2342/44: Melodram 27062

Symphony in E minor: RAI Symphony Orchestra of Milan (1968) Stradivarius 13610

BERLIOZ

Roméo et Juliette: Philadelphia Orchestra with Norman, Aler, Estes; Westminster Symphonic Choir (1986) EMI 7 47437 8

Symphonie fantastique: Philadelphia Orchestra (1984) EMI 7 474278 2

BRAHMS

Symphony No. 1: Philadelphia Orchestra (1989) Philips 426 299-2

Symphony No. 2: Philadelphia Orchestra (1988) Philips 423 334-2

Symphony No. 3: Philadelphia Orchestra (1989) Philips 426 253-2

Symphony No. 4: Philadelphia Orchestra (1988) Philips 422 337-2

Alto Rhapsody: Philadelphia Orchestra (1989) Philips 426 253-2

Tragic Overture: Philadelphia Orchestra (1988) Philips 422 337-2

Academic Festival Overture: Philadelphia Orchestra (1988) Philips 432 334-2

St. Anthony Variations: Philadelphia Orchestra (1989) Philips 426 299-2

Piano Concerto No. 1: Philadelphia Orchestra with Alexis Weissenberg, piano (1983) LP EMI 1435211

BRITTEN

Four Sea Interludes from *Peter Grimes:* RAI Symphony Orchestra of Milan (1968) Stradivarius 13610

BRUCKNER

Symphony No. 4, *Romantic:* Berlin Philharmonic (1985) EMI 7 47352 2

Symphony No. 6: Berlin Philharmonic (1988) EMI 7 49408 2

CHABRIER

España: Philadelphia Orchestra (1979) EMI 7 63572 2

CHERUBINI

Lodoïska: Popp, Vermillion, Ramey; Orchestra and Chorus of La Scala Sony Classical SLV SHV 46391

Mass for the Coronation of Charles X: Philharmonia Orchestra and Chorus (1984) EMI 7 49302 2*

Solemn Mass for the Coronation of Louis XVIII: London Philharmonic Orchestra and Chorus (1988) EMI 7 49553 2*

Requiem in C minor in Memory of Louis XVI: Ambrosian Singers, Philharmonia Orchestra (1980) EMI 7 49678 2*

Requiem in D minor: Ambrosian Singers, New Philharmonia Orchestra (1973) EMI 7 49301 2*

*These four choral works of Cherubini are available in a single set, EMI 7631612

CIMAROSA

Chi dell'altrui veste presto si spogli: Bruscantini, Montarsolo, Bonifacio, Bonisolli; Chorus of the Scarlatti Association of Naples, RAI Symphony Orchestra of Naples (1968) Nuova Era 3353/54

DONIZETTI

Don Pasquale: Bruscantini, Freni, Winbergh, Nucci; Ambrosian Opera Chorus, Philharmonia Orchestra (1982) EMI 7 47068 2

DVOŘÁK

Symphony No. 9, *From the New World*: New Philharmonia Orchestra (1976) LP EMI 069-02802

Concerto for Violin and Orchestra: Philadelphia Orchestra with Kyung-Wha Chung, violin (1988) EMI 7 49858 2

Romance for Violin and Orchestra: Philadelphia Orchestra with Kyung-Wha Chung, violin (1988) EMI 7 49858 2

FALLA

El sombrero de tres picos, Suites Nos. 1 and 2: Philadelphia Orchestra (1979) EMI 7 63572 2

FRANCK

Symphony in D major: Philadelphia Orchestra (1981) EMI 7 47849 2

Symphonic Poem, *Le chasseur maudit*: Philadelphia Orchestra (1981) EMI 7 47849 2

GLUCK

Orfeo ed Euridice: Baltsa, Marshall, Gruberova; Ambrosian Opera Chorus, Philharmonia Orchestra (1981) EMI 7 63637 2

HANDEL

Deborah: Norman, Lilowa, Anderko, Winkler, Cotrubas; Philharmonic Chorus of Prague, Orchestra of the Maggio Musicale Fiorentino (1970) Memories 4126

Water Music Suites: Berlin Philharmonic (1984) EMI 7 47145 2

HAYDN

Concerto for Trumpet and Orchestra in E minor: Philharmonia Orchestra with Maurice André, trumpet (1984) EMI 7 49474 2

Die Schöpfung: Popp, Araiza, Bar, Ramey; Vienna Philharmonic and Vienna State Opera Chorus (1992) Sony Classics laser disc SLV-46391

LEONCAVALLO

I Pagliacci: Scotto, Carreras, Nurmela, Benelli; Ambrosian Opera Chorus and Southend Boys Chorus, Philharmonia Orchestra (1979) EMI 736502 2

LISZT

Faust Symphony: Philadelphia Orchestra with Gösta Winbergh, Westminster Symphonic Choir (1982-83) LP EMI 1435703

Les Préludes: Philadelphia Orchestra (1982-83) EMI 7 47022 2

La campanella: Philharmonia Orchestra with Andrei Gavrilov, piano EMI 7 69125 2

MAHLER

Symphony No. 1: Philadelphia Orchestra (1984) EMI 7 47032 2

MASCAGNI

Cavalleria rusticana: Caballé, Carreras, Hamari, Varnay; Ambrosian Opera Chorus, Philharmonia Orchestra (1979) EMI 76365502 2

MENDELSSOHN

Symphony No. 3, *Scottish*: New Philharmonia Orchestra (1975) EMI 7 69660 2

Symphony No. 4, *Italian*: New Philharmonia Orchestra (1976) EMI 7 69660 2

Symphony No. 5, *Reformation*: New Philharmonia Orchestra (1979) LP EMI 069-03726

Overture, *Meeresstille und glückliche Fahrt*: New Philharmonia Orchestra (1975) LP EMI 069-02731

MOZART

Così fan tutte: Marshall, Baltsa, Araiza, Morris, Battle, van Dam; Vienna Opera Chorus, Vienna Philharmonic (1982) EMI 7 69580 2

Le nozze di Figaro: Price, Battle, Murray, Hynninen, Allen, Rydl, Vienna Opera Chorus, Vienna Philharmonic (1986) EMI 7 47978 8

Requiem, K. 626: Pace, Meier, Lopardo, Morris; Swedish Radio Chorus, Stockholm Chamber Choir, Berlin Philharmonic (1987) and *Ave verum corpus*, K. 618: Swedish Radio Chorus and Berlin Philharmonic (1987) EMI 7 49640 2

Piano Concerto No. 22, K. 482: Philharmonia Orchestra with Sviatoslav Richter, piano (1979) EMI 7 69013 2

Violin Concerto No. 2, K. 211: Philharmonia Orchestra with Anne-Sophie Mutter, violin (1981) EMI 7 47011 2

Violin Concerto No. 4. K. 218: Philharmonia Orchestra with Anne-Sophie Mutter, violin (1981) EMI 7 47011 2

Symphony No. 24, K. 182: Philharmonia Orchestra (1982) LP EMI 1435 281

Symphony No. 25, K. 183: New Philharmonia Orchestra (1976) LP EMI 063-02838

Symphony No. 29, K. 201: New Philharmonia Orchestra (1976) LP EMI 063-02838

Symphony No. 41, K. 551, *Jupiter:* Berlin Philharmonic (1985) EMI 7 47465 2

Divertimento, K. 136: Berlin Philharmonic (1988) EMI 7 47465

MUSSORGSKY/RAVEL

Pictures at an Exhibition: Philadelphia Orchestra (1978) EMI 7 47099 2

ORFF

Carmina Burana : Auger, Summers, van Kesteren; Southend Boys Chorus, Philharmonia Orchestra (1979) EMI 7 47100 2

PERGOLESI

Lo frate'nnamorato: Felle, Focile, Corbelli, de Simone, di Nissa; Orchestra of La Scala (1991) EMI 7 54240 2

PROKOFIEV

Ivan the Terrible: Arkhipova, Mokrenko, Morgunov; Ambrosian Opera Chorus, Philharmonia Orchestra (1977) EMI 7 69584

Romeo and Juliet, Suites Nos. 1 and 2: Philadelphia Orchestra (1981) EMI 7 47004 2

Sinfonietta, Op. 5/48: Philharmonia Orchestra (1977) LP EMI 167-02966/67

Symphony No. 5: Philadelphia Orchestra (1990) Philips 432 083-2

Symphonic Poem, *Meeting of the Volga and the Don:* Philadelphia Orchestra (1990) Philips 432 083-2

RACHMANINOFF

Piano Concerto No. 2: Philadelphia Orchestra with Andrei Gavrilov, piano (1991) EMI 7 49966 2

Piano Concerto No. 3: Philadelphia Orchestra with Andrei Gavrilov, piano (1986) EMI 7 49049 2

RAVEL

Alborada del gracioso: Philadelphia Orchestra (1982) LP EMI 069-43268

Boléro: Philadelphia Orchestra (1982) EMI 7 47022 2

Daphnis et Chloé, Suite No. 2: Philadelphia Orchestra, Singing City Choir, (1982) LP EMI 069-43268

Rapsodie espagnole: Philadelphia Orchestra (1979) EMI 63572 2

Concerto for the Left Hand: Orchestra Teatro Comunale di Genova with Sviatoslav Richter, piano (1979) Stradivarius 10024/5/6

RESPIGHI

Feste romane: Philadelphia Orchestra (1984) EMI 7 47316 2

Fontane di Roma: Philadelphia Orchestra (1984) EMI 7 47316 2

Pini di Roma: Philadelphia Orchestra (1984) EMI 7 47316 2

RIMSKY-KORSAKOV

Scheherazade: Philadelphia Orchestra (1982) EMI 7 47023 2

RODRIGO

Concerto di Aranjez: RAI Symphony Orchestra of Milano with Narciso Yepes, guitar (1968) Stradivarius 13610

ROSSINI

Guillaume Tell: Zancanaro, Merritt, Surjan, Terranova, Roni, Studer; Chorus and Orchestra of La Scala (1988) Philips 422 391-2

Stabat mater: Malfitano, Baltsa, Gambill, Howell; Chorus and Orchestra of Maggio Musicale Fiorentino (1981) EMI 7 47402 2

Overtures to *Il barbiere di Siviglia*; *La scala di seta*; *Guillaume Tell*; *Semiramide*; *L'assedio di Corinto*; *Il viaggio a Reims*: Philharmonia Orchestra (1980) EMI 7 47118 2

SAINT-SAËNS

Piano Concerto No. 4: RAI Symphony Orchestra of Milan with Robert Casadesus, piano (1968) Stradivarius 13610

SCARLATTI

La dirindina: Ravaglia, Bonisolli, Bruscantini; RAI Scarlatti Orchestra of Naples (1968) Nuova Era 3353/54

SCHUBERT

Symphony No. 1: Vienna Philharmonic EMI 7 54066 2

Symphony No. 3: Vienna Philharmonic (1988) EMI 7 49850 2

Symphony No. 4, *Tragic*: Vienna Philharmonic (1987) EMI 7 49724 2

Symphony No. 5: Vienna Philharmonic (1988) EMI 7 49850 2

Symphony No. 6: Vienna Philharmonic (1987) EMI 7 49724 2

Symphony No. 8, *Unfinished*: Vienna Philharmonic EMI 7 54066 2

Symphony No. 9, *Great C major*: Vienna Philharmonic (1986) EMI 7 47697 2

SCHUMANN

Symphony No. 1, *Spring*: Philharmonia Orchestra (1978) LP EMI 069-03721

Symphony No. 2: Philharmonia Orchestra (1977) LP EMI 069-03406

Symphony No. 3, *Rhenish*: Philharmonia Orchestra (1977) LP EMI 069-03407

Symphony No. 4: Philharmonia Orchestra (1976) LP EMI 069-02876

Violin Concerto in D major: Philharmonia Orchestra with Gidon Kremer (1976) EMI 7 47110 2

Overture, *Die Braut von Messina*: Philharmonia Orchestra (1977) LP EMI 069-03407

Overture, *Hermann und Dorothea*: Philharmonia Orchestra (1977) LP EMI C 069-03406

SHOSTAKOVICH

Symphony No. 13, *Babi Yar*: RAI Chorus and Orchestra of Rome (1970) Memories 4101

SIBELIUS

Violin Concerto: Philharmonia Orchestra with Gidon Kremer (1982) EMI 7 47110 2

SCRIABIN

Symphony No. 1: Philadelphia Orchestra with Stefania Toczyska, mezzo-soprano; Michael Myers, tenor; Westminster Symphonic Choir (1985) EMI 7 47349 2

Symphony No. 2: Philadelphia Orchestra (1989) EMI 7 49859 2

Symphony No. 3, *Le Divin poème*: Philadelphia Orchestra (1988) EMI 7 49115 2

Prométhée, le poème de feu: Philadelphia Orchestra (1989) EMI 7 54112 2

Le Poème de l'extase: Philadelphia Orchestra (1989) EMI 7 64061

SPONTINI

Agnes von Hohenstaufen: Caballé, Stella, Prevedi, Guelfi, Bruscantini; RAI Symphony Orchestra and Chorus of Rome (1970) Memories 4104/05; Foyer 2029

STRAUSS

Aus Italien: Berlin Philharmonic (1989) Philips 422-399 2

Aus Italien: RAI Symphony Orchestra of Milan (1968) Nuova Era 2296

Don Juan: Berlin Philharmonic (1989) Philips 422-399 2

STRAVINSKY

Suite, *L'Oiseau de feu*: Philadelphia Orchestra (1978) EMI 7 47099 2

Petrushka: Philadelphia Orchestra (1981) EMI 7 47408 2

Le Sacre du printemps: Philadelphia Orchestra (1978) EMI 7 47048 2

TCHAIKOVSKY

Symphony No. 1, *Winter Dreams*: New Philharmonia Orchestra (1975) EMI 7 47866 2

Symphony No. 2, *Little Russian*: New Philharmonia Orchestra (1977) EMI 7 47867 2

Symphony No. 3, *Polish*: Philharmonia Orchestra (1977) EMI 7 47868

Symphony No. 4: Philharmonia Orchestra (1978) EMI 7 47860 2

Symphony No. 4: Philadelphia Orchestra (1990) EMI 7 54112 2

Symphony No. 5: Philharmonia Orchestra (1978) EMI 7 47859 2

Symphony No. 6: Philharmonia Orchestra (1979) EMI 7 47858 2

Symphony No. 6: Philadelphia Orchestra (1989) EMI 7 64061 2

Manfred Symphony: Philharmonia Orchestra (1982) EMI 7 47412

Fantasy-Overture, *Hamlet*: Philadelphia Orchestra (1989) EMI 7 49858 2

Fantasy-Overture, *Romeo and Juliet*: Philharmonia Orchestra (1977) EMI 7 47867 2

Fantasy-Overture, *Romeo and Juliet*: Philadelphia Orchestra (1988) EMI 7 49115 2

Overture, *1812*: Philadelphia Orchestra EMI 7 47022 2

Ballet Suite, *Sleeping Beauty*: Philadelphia Orchestra (1984) EMI 7 47075 2

Ballet Suite, *Swan Lake*: Philadelphia Orchestra (1984) EMI 7 47075 2

Serenade for Strings: Philadelphia Orchestra (1981) LP EMI 069-03970

Piano Concerto No. 1: Philharmonia Orchestra with Andrei Gavrilov (1979) EMI 7 69125 2

TELEMANN

Trumpet Concerto in D major: Philharmonia Orchestra with Maurice André, trumpet (1984) EMI 7 47311 2

TORELLI

Trumpet Concerto in D major: Philharmonia Orchestra with Maurice André, trumpet (1984) EMI 7 47311 2

VERDI

Aida: Hillebrand, Fassbaender, Tomowa-Sintow, Domingo, Lloyd, Nimsgern, Orth, Seibel; Bavarian Opera Chorus, Bavarian Orchestra (1979) LP Legendary Recordings 174

Aida: Caballé, Domingo, Cossotto, Cappuccilli, Ghiaurov, Chorus of Covent Garden, New Philharmonia Orchestra (1974) EMI 7 47271 2

Attila: Raimondi, Stella, Cechele, Guelfi, Ferrari, Monreale; RAI Symphony Orchestra and Chorus of Rome (1970) Memories 4178/79

Attila: Ramey, Studer, Shicoff, Zancanaro, Gavazzi, Surjan; Chorus and Orchestra of La Scala (1989) EMI 7 49952 2

Un ballo in maschera: Arroyo, Domingo, Cappuccilli, Cossotto, Grisi; Chorus of Covent Garden, New Philharmonia Orchestra (1975) EMI 7 69576 2

Ernani: Domingo, Freni, Bruson, Ghiaurov, Michieli; Chorus and Orchestra of La Scala (1982) EMI 7 47083 2

La forza del destino: Freni, Zajic, Domingo, Zancanaro, Plishka, Bruscantini; Chorus and Orchestra of La Scala (1986) EMI 7 47485 8

Macbeth: Cossotto, Milnes, Raimondi, Carreras; Ambrosian Opera Chorus, New Philharmonia Orchestra (1976) EMI 479548

I Masnadieri: Cioni, Montefusco, Maragliano, Formighini; Chorus and Orchestra Maggio Musicale Fiorentino (1969) Hunt 580

Nabucco: Manuguerra, Scotto, Ghiaurov, Luchetti, Obratsova; Ambrosian Opera Chorus, Philharmonia Orchestra (1977-78) EMI 7 47488 2

Rigoletto: La Scola, Dessì, Zancanaro, Burchuladze, Senn; Chorus and Orchestra of La Scala (1988) EMI 7 49605 2

La traviata: Scotto, Kraus, Bruson, Walker, Buchan; Ambrosian Opera Chorus, Marine Band, Philharmonia Orchestra (1980) EMI 7 47538 8

Il trovatore: Cossutta, Cruz-Romo, Cossotto, Manuguerra, Ferrin, Matteini; Chorus and Orchestra Maggio Musicale Fiorentino (1978) LP HRE 817

I vespri siciliani: Studer, Merritt, Zancanaro, Furlanetto; Chorus and Orchestra of La Scala (1989) EMI 7 54043 2

Quattro pezzi sacri: Arleen Auger, soprano; Swedish Radio Chorus and Stockholm Chamber Choir, Berlin Philharmonic (1982) EMI 7 47066 2

Requiem: Scotto, Lucchetti, Nesterenko; Ambrosian Opera Chorus, Philharmonia Orchestra (1979) LP EMI 167 03653/4

Requiem: Studer, Zajic, Pavarotti, Ramey; Chorus and Orchestra of La Scala (1987) EMI 7 49390 2

Overtures to *Aida, Macbeth, I vespri siciliani*: Philharmonia Orchestra LP EMI 069-03972

Choruses from *Aida, I Lombardi alla prima Crociata, Macbeth, Nabucco, Il trovatore*; *Ernani*: Ambrosian Opera Chorus and Chorus of Covent Garden; New Philharmonia Orchestra and Philharmonia Orchestra LP EMI 069-03953

Overtures to *La battaglia di Legnano, La forza del destino, Giovanna d'Arco; Luisa Miller, Nabucco*: New Philharmonia Orchestra LP EMI 069-02877

Overtures, Choruses, and ballet music from *Nabucco, I Lombardi alla prima Crociata; Macbeth, Il trovatore, I vespri siciliani, La*

forza del destino, Aida: Ambrosian Opera Chorus and Chorus of Covent Garden, New Philharmonia Orchestra and Philharmonia Orchestra EMI 7 47274 2

VIVALDI

Gloria, RV 589: Teresa Berganza, mezzo-soprano; Lucia Valentini Terrani, contralto: Philharmonia Orchestra and Chorus (1977) EMI 7 47990 2

Magnificat, RV 611: Teresa Berganza, mezzo-soprano; Lucia Valentini Terrani, contralto; Philharmonia Orchestra and Chorus (1976) EMI 7 47990 2

RECORDED, NOT YET RELEASED IN U.S.A.

HAYDN

The Seven Last Words of Our Saviour on the Cross: Berlin Philharmonic

LEONCAVALLO

Pagliacci with Pavarotti, Dessi, Pons, Coni, Gavazzi, Westminster Symphonic Choir, Philadelphia Boys Choir, Philadelphia Orchestra (Philips)

MOZART

Symphony No. 40; Symphony No. 36, *Linz*: Vienna Philharmonic (1st recording of complete cycle of Mozart symphonies)

Symphony No. 40, Symphony No. 41: Vienna Philharmonic, live from 1991 Salzburg Festival (laserdisc only)

MUSSORGSKY/RAVEL

Pictures at an Exhibition; *Night on Bald Mountain*: Philadelphia Orchestra (Philips)

PROKOFIEV

Symphony No. 3: Symphony No. 1, *Classical*: Philadelphia Orchestra (Philips)

PUCCINI

Tosca with Vaness, Giacomini, Zancanaro, Serraiocco, Westminster Choir, Philadelphia Boys Choir, Philadelphia Orchestra (Philips)

TCHAIKOVSKY

Symphony No. 5; *Francesca da Rimini*: Philadelphia Orchestra (EMI)

The Philadelphia Orchestra, 1972–92

William Smith,
Associate Conductor

First Violins
Norman Carol, Concertmaster
David Arben
Nancy Bean
Jonathan Beiler
Frank Costanzo
Cathleen O'Carroll Dalschaert
William de Pasquale
Ernest L. Goldstein
Barbara Govatos
Julia Grayson
Larry Grika
Arnold Grossi
David Grunschlag
Herold Klein
Herbert Light
Owen Lusak
Max Miller
Hirono Oka
Laura Park
Charles Rex
Paul Roby
Frank E. Saam
Vladimir Shapiro
Morris Shulik
Barbara Sorlien
Vera Tarnowsky

Second Violins
Paul Arnold
Boris Balter
Luis Biava*
Norman Black
Davyd Booth
Stephane Dalschaert
Robert de Pasquale
Armand Di Camillo
George Dreyfus
Kimberly Fisher
Yoko Gilbert
Virginia Halfmann
Philip Kates
Joseph Lanza
Louis Lanza
Dmitri Levin
Irving Ludwig
Michael Ludwig
Irvin Rosen
Booker Rowe
Isadore Schwartz
Yumi Ninomiya Scott
Jerome Wigler
Cynthia Williams

Violas
Leonard Bogdanoff
Gabriel Braverman
Donald R. Clauser
Patrick Connolly
Sidney Curtiss
Joseph de Pasquale*
Renard Edwards
Christian Euler
James Fawcett
Albert Filosa
Judy Geist
Wolfgang Granat
Charles Griffin
Leonard Mogill
Gaetano Molieri
Irving Segall

Cellos
Ohad Bar-David
Robert Cafaro
Santo Caserta
Francis de Pasquale
Gloria de Pasquale
Joseph Druian
Marcel Farago
Harry Gorodetzer
Barbara Haffner
Richard Harlow
George Harpham
Patricia Weimer Hess
John Koen
Samuel Mayes
Winifred Mayes
Sang-Min Park
Bert Phillips
Kathryn Picht
Deborah Reeder
Christopher Rex
William Saputelli
Lloyd Smith
William Stokking*
Peter Stumpf

Basses
Wilfred Batchelder
Curtis Burris
Neil Courtney
David Fay
Samuel Gorodetzer
Emilio Gravagno
John Hood
Robert Kesselman
Peter Lloyd
Ferdinand Maresh
Duane Rosengard

Henry Scott
Roger M. Scott*
Michael Shahan
Carl Torello

Flutes
David Cramer
Jeffrey Khaner*
John C. Krell
Loren N. Lind
Murray W. Panitz
Kenneth E. Scutt
Kenton F. Terry
Kazuo Tokito

Oboes
Jonathan Blumenfeld
Cynthia Koledo DeAlmeida
John de Lancie
Stevens Hewitt
Charles M. Morris
Louis Rosenblatt
Peter Smith
Richard Woodhams*

Clarinets
Anthony M. Gigliotti*
Donald Montanaro
Raoul Querze
Ronald Reuben

Bassoons
Adelchi Louis Angelucci
Bernard Garfield*
Mark Gigliotti
Robert J. Pfeuffer
Richard Ranti
John Shamlian

Horns
Kendall Betts
Randy Gardner
Martha Glaze
Glenn Janson
Mason Jones
Jeffry Kirschen
Nolan Miller*
Herbert Pierson
John Simonelli
Howard Wall
David Wetherill*
Daniel Williams

Trumpets
Roger Blackburn
Robert W. Earley
Gilbert Johnson
Frank Kaderabek*
Samuel Krauss
Donald E. McComas
Calvin C. Price
Seymour Rosenfeld

Trombones
Joseph Alessi
Blair Bollinger
Tyrone Breuninger
Eric Carlson
Glenn Dodson*
Robert S. Harper
M. Dee Stewart
Charles Vernon

Tuba
Paul Krzywicki

Timpani
Michael Bookspan
Gerald Carlyss
Don S. Liuzzi*

Percussion
Alan Abel
Michael Bookspan*
Anthony Orlando

Harps
Marilyn Costello*
Margarita Csonka Montanaro

Librarians
Nancy M. Bradburd
Anthony Ciccarelli
Robert M. Grossman
Clinton F. Nieweg*
Jesse C. Taynton

Stage Personnel
Edward Barnes
Edward Barnes, Jr.*
Theodore Hauptle
James J. Sweeney
James J. Sweeney, Jr.

*Current Principal

THE PHILADELPHIA ORCHESTRA ASSOCIATION, 1972–92

ENDLEAF QUOTE: FROM
A SPEECH AT THE DINNER
HONORING RETIRED
PHILADELPHIA ORCHES-
TRA MEMBERS, 1991